D0363527

Big Snake
Little Snake

Big Snake
Little Snake

An Inquiry into Risk

DBC PIERRE

CHEERIO

CHEERIO

First published in Great Britain in 2022 by
Cheerio Publishing
www.cheeriopublishing.com
info@cheeriopublishing.com

10 9 8 7 6 5 4 3 2 1

Typeset in Garamond by MacGuru Ltd
Printed and bound in Great Britain by
Clays Ltd, Elcograf S.p.A.

A CIP catalogue record for this book is available from the British Library.

ISBN 978 1 78816 977 6
eISBN 978 1 78283 949 1
Audio ISBN 978 1 80081 148 5

I think risk is too strong a word.
Francis Bacon

Contents

The scenes that follow are real.
Some are ridiculous but that's reality for you.
I used to make up lies less ridiculous.
This is probably why I stopped.

Why Little Snake

The season of this inquiry was long and tropical. A pair of Caribbean years with a posse of colleagues who made every day a brassy reggae – though they would lecture me now for not saying calypso or soca, as none are Jamaican. But the point is the rhythm was hot and clunky and gleaming with heart-shine. And these times also saw me make a short commercial film. I had decided it should feature a parrot. This was a dumb idea. This is what happens when ideas from your desk meet the Great Outdoors. I call it the ballistic chaos of maths outside the window. In short: reality. And that's what our inquiry is for: to ask if it's truly chaos or *intuitive order*. To see if we can make chaos our friend. And to flip a passing finger at all the metrics being used to scare us away from life.

It's time to remind ourselves what really goes on.

And that it's okay.

Not thus but anyway, I came to Trinidad & Tobago: seductive twin-island republic with enough crackling life to deserve a planet of its own. I had phoned about a visa from my living room with the radio blaring and the embassy official who answered the call simply said: 'Puccini at this hour of the morning?' – and I liked the place already.

The descent of a wide-bodied jet onto Tobago feels like the loudest thing to happen there since the island burst from the sea. Beyond immigration, which was woody and vaguely damp in the way of a place that's blasé about coconuts, the terminal led to a little concrete courtyard under a roof. It had some tables and was rimmed by waxy greenery where thieving birds were stirring the leaves. A window in a hut at one end offered drinks and snacks. I got a drink and phoned my colleagues in Port of Spain, on the larger adjacent island of Trinidad, before going to catch the short flight over.

'I'm in Tobago,' I told them.

'Watch out for Ramona!' they said. And this is how our inquiry begins. 'Watch out for Ramona!' An immediate introduction to odds long and short. Looking back, the words were a clue that I might soon be meeting a lifestyle that probability could never predict. A whole climate of life which resists calculation on paper, a universal organic lifestyle as real as the sweet bang of heat at the aircraft door. Looking back to those early hours on the islands, they were a reception to something far bigger than metrics, to a nature we must have known but have forgotten, a drawer containing a candle and matches in a stranger's darkened farm.

I wandered to the perimeter fence and squinted down the runway. It ran onto the narrow sandy strip of a good surfing beach, Crown Point, known for its clean right-handed barrels. The waves were said to be inconsistent, though, governed as they were by unclear odds. A veteran Marine I knew used to access naval weather-buoy data online where he could see big sets forming when they were still a day or more out. He would drop everything and sail over to catch the waves. None of this explained Ramona but, as it happened, the turboprop to Trinidad was running six hours late, so there was time to sit and wonder and be charmed by the birds.

Tropical bird calls have echo and reverb and are clearly run through an amp; so thriving is this place that bursts with fruit and sex that the calls of tropical birds create a studio-quality soundscape compared to the busking birds back home.

Ramona was a foreigner who claimed she had caught AIDS from a local as a tourist to the island some time before – the word was out that she was back for revenge, on a spree to pass it on wherever she could. Heinous Ramona!

Between the snack bar and the perimeter fence over the six hours of that delay I could only ponder the flowering odds. How many people could she sleep with? How was that going to work? I didn't know how many people lived on Tobago but it wasn't many, maybe sixty thousand, compared to Trinidad's million-plus. Of that sixty thousand the percentage of people who were of an age to succumb to Ramona – not accounting for Ramona's unknown tastes and tolerances – might be a third of the population at most. Exclude the very young and very old, also those who were otherwise engaged and out of sight, unable to sample her deadly charms. Plus let's be practical and take into account that a certain number within that third of candidates would abstain for fear of being discovered and killed by their current partners, much more quickly than Ramona could do it.

Another lazy drink from the snack-bar window. New birds came round to scavenge in the sun. So that's nominally twenty thousand candidates minus six thousand six hundred and sixty-six, let's say, who simply don't have eyes for Ramona. From that number another third will be religious or otherwise clean living and decent, unmoved by her enticements; so we're left with a pool of eight thousand eight hundred and eighty-eight. But Tobago not being that big – in fact the ideal size to film the original *Swiss Family Robinson* on, you could walk the length of the island in a day – so that eight-plus thousand won't all be out at once. The capital, Scarborough, has barely twice that number in total. Half the people of Tobago's capital will not be out waiting for Ramona.

But some will. To calculate the maths for red-blooded targets on the streets and beaches we'll be conservative and divide this number by ten. Eight hundred and eighty-eight circulating targets in a laid-back population of sixty thousand. But now: the news had clearly reached Trinidad. So Ramona is already being hunted. I'm going to divide again by ten, to eighty-eight useful people, because Ramona is up against time. Plus Ramona is European, I think, which is unusual against the general population, the vast majority of which is Afro-Trinidadian or Tobagonian. And Ramona has to identify two groups within that wider population: those who haven't heard the news and those who don't care. How quickly she can seduce and sleep with members of these target groups is key, and also implies how fast she can negotiate a short-term-no-ties bang, as well as disengage from previous conquests. All this within the unknown time-frame of a police hunt.

Ramona has to get cracking.

These calculations under flowering trees take nothing away from the story's violence. Thoughts chime around like bird calls, and not even thoughts but mind-maps, feelings, trans-dimensional grids, operations beyond risk calculation. We don't know the numbers so we can't call the odds – *is this life?* – but what's certain is that there will be an outcome, predictable or not. And our specific mission is to look at that space between odds and their outcome. We've grown obsessed with predicting numbers without getting any better at it, and it seems to me that the space between events not happening and events having happened is down to more than just mathematical probability. We can even sense the maths is incomplete; but we cling on to the belief that if this incompleteness can't be modelled on a computer it doesn't exist. When we feel instinctively that the opposite might be true but we just don't have the numbers.

Abiogenesis is the name given to the electro-chemical process by which life erupts from inanimate matter. The so-called spark of life. It's the accepted scientific model for the creation of life on Earth, but how it actually happens is not really known. Theories tell us no more than we can observe: that it's an *energy*. Science knows which elements can cause it, it knows what happens once it's been caused. But it can't say where that spark comes from.

The Ramona news faded away shortly after arriving on Trinidad. I think she was found and deported to face justice in her homeland. Meanwhile, not too far from the coast in north-western Trinidad, a short drive from Port of Spain, an impulse passed between states to spark this inquiry.

It came to my doorstep as a little snake.

Snake Charming in Jungle and Mangrove

To begin let's recall that there are estimated to be almost nine million species of living things on Earth. We think we may have identified just over a million of them so far. The rest are a mystery. This is where we really stand despite our fancy maths. It means the background odds for embarking on our inquiry – that is the odds of being born human – start at nearly nine million to one. The odds of being born a manicou must also be nine million to one, as they must for ending up as a type of little snake. Thus in reading this today on Earth you have already beaten odds in the range of trillions to one against, and probably much more. We find ourselves both in this situation. Then another trillion unique chances brought us to intersect right now on this page, as opposed to tomorrow or next year or much more likely never. It matters here because the world we're setting out to question will not take those odds into account. It will wait until just now and say to all of us at once: 'Your odds of being bitten by a snake are one in a hundred and thirty.' And when we add this to the odds of dying in a car (one in ninety), a tornado (one in sixty thousand), a fire (one in two hundred and fifty) or a shark attack (one in eight million), we may as well stay in bed. Though that can kill us too.

But we mysteriously survive. Not bitten by the snake. Not hit by the tornado, although we know some people are. But every day that we're not killed by a train or a bull or an asteroid event seems a huge disproof of the application of odds to humans. So: should we wonder if it's due to those odds being disconnected from a maths stream that began with our not having been born the snake?

However it is, it's not damn good enough, is where we're headed. Because having been born a *Homo sapien* on a planet in a cosmos with no other visible life at all, our perception of probability may not have been updated since it was first written down on papyrus.

And we're not out to trash science: our lust for prediction is natural and human (even science would admit that), and this inquiry is also a lust for prediction (it would add); and is itself mildly scientific, if more adapted for reflection over drinks.

So to business: most predictions aim to create a benefit, which makes our inquiry about risk. We might well ask: what is risk? And for this we need to split the inquiry in two. Think of a stage scenario: the background is an infinite jungle of risks where probabilities flick around like animals, none of which we can see, the jungle is dark to us, there are obscene hoots and cries but no creatures appear until they suddenly do. While here in the foreground are the mangroves of risks we're aware of and can possibly calculate.

Risk in this foreground is an equation of likelihood and impact: how likely is something to happen, how great is the impact if it does, what is the cost if it doesn't? This is the area of risk that covers gambling. It unites the arenas of cockroach racing – with legendary roaches like the giant *Destructo* whose career was ended early when somebody stepped on it – with dog, horse and camel racing, as well as casino and table games. But now: let's propose that this foreground of visible risks is connected through nature to the jungle behind. That this foreground of risk, chance and probability is the protruding hand of that jungle, an amoebic protrusion into our consciousness of risks we can see and assess. And it also has layers: one of odds subject to human or animal influence, another of straight mathematical chances. The question of whether strictly probabilistic gambles such as roulette are equal to running live agents like horses through variables of biology, physics and training is a good one. Live agents like the giant roach *Destructo* shortened odds with their prowess and talent but there is no prowess and talent in a roulette wheel. Those are naked chances. Odds have to be guessed for one and are absolute for the other, but neither system will tell you which number or which cockroach will win. That outcome lives in the deepest jungle of chaos where it's mathematically unlikely in the history of the universe that a deck of cards has shuffled the same way twice, and as unlikely one ever will. National lotteries all swarm to set up shop around this effect, selling crappier odds than dying in a honeybee attack.

But we're onto them. This panorama of imaginary maths

is now placed centre stage in our inquiry's setting. Sure it's not maths-maths but snake-maths, a background and foreground of writhing coils, since, truth be told, we're not here for arithmetic but snake charming.

But onwards. Just keep a sharp eye on the jungle behind.

Background to Little Snake

Snakes, I've seen a few. A couple have gone by me in the nearby wild, winding along on their mission of staining our psyches. And I have one big snake story to share. At about four years old, maybe five, I was volunteered into this little story. My mother volunteered me as 'man of the house', since my father was out at work. I featured alongside an Eastern Brown Snake, the second-most venomous terrestrial snake in the world after the Inland Taipan. A snake allegedly responsible for sixty per cent of snakebite deaths in its area of operation. A lightning-fast six-foot snake that can outrun an adult sprinting, a snake that rises up and spreads its jaws when confronted, one with a proud record of felling its victims in minutes using clinical tools of haemorrhage and cardiac arrest.

Otherwise it was a modest snake without swagger. Our

pairing in the story was apt because neither it nor I knew its statistics in detail. It didn't know it had a sixty per cent kill rate in its area of operation. Neither did I. Our casting in this sense was inspired, more Euro cinema than Hollywood, where the boy would have had to be eerily articulate and the snake foretold by a legend. Euro cinema grasps that a snake is more sinister for being dull and slim. A brown snake with almost invisible fangs. So I met this snake in the old stone winery-homestead I was born into, which had stone stairs leading down to a wine cellar. The stairs were between the kitchen and a sunroom where as a toddler I once had a fever dream about being visited and cared for by an airline cabin crew.

It meant that this area around the cellar stairs, home to such a warm dream, was a benign territory in my mind. A wide corridor between kitchen and sunroom formed the beam of a T whose shaft was a hall running the length of the house. The cellar stairwell looked down that hall and diagonally faced a pantry on the opposite wall. A junction of major activity.

Back in this rambling stone house a cast of my mother, my sister and her bestie were going about their day; the friend like a second sister who was perky and good in ways only seen on TV. This young friend went to a kitchen cupboard that day, found an iguana's tail among the products, yanked it – and it turned out to be the brown snake of our story. She was lucky: out it flew and went to ground in the pantry across the hall. But then we all thronged at a distance trying to spot it, which made it unsettled. After a while it bolted to the cellar stairs.

It didn't go down into the cellar but stayed halfway up on

a stair looking back. Within one flying strike. Not happy. My mother meanwhile decided she would call my father at work. He was at the university half an hour or more away, but she had this brainwave for me: I would fetch my little wooden chair, my activities chair, stand it at the top of the stairs and *make sure the snake didn't come up.*

'Make sure it doesn't come up,' she said. I watched the snake as I sat on the chair and the snake watched me back with its tongue. For all I knew the snake's mother had sent it to make sure I didn't go down because we watched each other from equally pointless positions, positions at odds with most of our goals and tastes in life, and especially our desires for that moment. Instead of pursuing our aims under any system of predetermination, intelligent free will or mystical destiny, we sat wondering what the fuck was going to happen when one of us made a move. The answer was that this snake would pump enough venom into me to melt the circulatory system of a calf, whereas I would throw a small wooden chair. Neither of us knew this at the time, although in a way we also did: the snake was primed to strike by default, and I was ready to target the snake with the chair.

Aside from being possibly melted internally I remember the moment being uncomfortable for another reason. A vague sense that I was growing up into a world where things didn't have to make sense. It made no sense to guard the snake. I mean, how was this going to work? Would the sound of my lifeless body hitting the deck let everyone know the snake had come up? Granted: this is the Health & Safety viewpoint and things are never as bad as that. Snakes won't look for trouble, and I knew that, I knew not to make sudden moves. Now looking back I can even superimpose a romantic trope, the noble savage snake and I in an instinctual pact beyond understanding, a bond of innocent respect, Claude Rains and Humphrey Bogart at the end of *Casablanca*.

My father came in, took up a rifle and shot the snake's head clean off. The body and head danced around for a long time, the head like a mouse trailing blood. I didn't know what to feel. It had been minding its own business before we flushed it out, this snake. The odds of it being disturbed had been long, given where brown snakes like to rest. They're not a showy snake. They're introverts who hide and make venom and love. Odds were very long that anyone would pull a brown snake's tail by accident. But the odds shortened up when the snake entered a zone of opposable thumbs. Always tugging and pulling, thumbs never stop. The odds of being bitten indoors were also pretty long, but they shortened for every second you spent within sight of an uncomfortable snake. Later I heard they never die until sundown. Doesn't matter when you kill them. And I respect that.

Among my recurring dreams since then are snakebite dreams.

But not cabin-crew dreams.

This is the power of snakes.

Setting for Little Snake

Take a raw chicken leg and hold it like a hammer by the drumstick. Bash the thigh end on a hard surface until it flanges like an anvil. Then take the leg, with the drumstick below and pointed left, and lay it down as if to kiss the top of South America's head. This is how you arrive at the shape of Trinidad. It's in a sixty-nine with Venezuela whose coast points a gun at the uppermost thigh while the drumstick points one back. A place so thriving with power that it didn't need to be shaped like a noble fighting beast. It has ocelots and can take any form it likes. Trinidad has for most intents and purposes also eradicated racial disharmony by blending all its peoples through every permutation. These have then spun music and life through all permutations until a match will strike on thin air.

Under the left-hand flange of the anvil-head, facing Venezuela across the Gulf of Paria, lies Port of Spain, shimmering and clattering. Here I plotted to make a short commercial film with a parrot. Ten minutes away up the steep jungled slope of a mountain range was perched the house where I lived. The place had three storeys. It could've had more for how steep it was set into this hill with fruit and creatures and a neighbour who I caught in my tree stealing coconuts. He was welcome to them and had worked this out by himself. There were also little mangos growing wild in tall grass behind this modernist house. A big clean cement house that was empty because I couldn't afford anything to put in it, but that suited modernism anyway. It had a stereo and a fridge. A spiral stair wound down to a bar room overlooking the valley below. If anyone came around we sat on the floor. It was carpeted with tight tan carpeting, but not so fancy that beer couldn't sometimes spill. A view plunged through windows over the opposite side of the valley with a road running far below past a mini-mall with a pizza place. To the left the coastline spat islands called Dragon's Teeth across the muddy gulf to Venezuela.

Fireflies came around at night flashing green at the speed of airport tugs. They also came inside, which is when I discovered a gap big enough to push a lawnmower through between the tops of the walls and the roof. Mower with the handles folded anyway. There was also therefore a bat which made its rounds at night up near the ceiling; not one of your frenzied flying mice but a larger and more stereotypical bat. These gaps between wall and roof helped circulate air, they made life breezy, and anyway the ceilings were so high – this was a double-mezzanined place – that nobody would even get a lawnmower up there.

Little Snake headquarters. Find a patch of carpet, here we go.

The Actual Little Snake

Hammering like a stunt pilot up the steep bastard driveway before gravity tossed the car back into the valley was my last memory before Little Snake. Once the scene had passed into history it became the last scene upon which any probabilities for the rest of my life could be drawn. Thankfully I hadn't died from the forces of gravity. I was yet to meet Little Snake, so I was still calculating my odds for future trips up the driveway against the host of background odds for all the days of my future.

The road itself was long and steep and grew steeper as you rose. Then you hit the hillside proper with this one last house perched up it beside which someone had thought to put a driveway like a ski ramp. It hooked sharply behind the house at the end onto a small patch of acceptably flat concrete. The trick was to toss the car up and around that corner. You had to drop gear and gun it from about a hundred yards down the road or you wouldn't make it up, you'd stall and slide back, which I'd only done once. You only do this once. And you can't park at the top half of the street and walk the rest of the way, as the slope would test your handbrake. On top of this the place suffers thundering earthquakes.

I made it safely up this time and got out of the car at the back of the house where it's more or less level ground. Perhaps I thought of parrots for the film. Perhaps I thought of Giulietta Masina in *La Strada*. I came in the little gate and along a tiled walkway that led to the main door. This door had an iron cage over it, decorative but for security. As I unlocked it I looked down and there was a little snake on the doormat. Now, the island has some evil snakes aside from the boa constrictors they call *macajuels*, whose young are occasionally heard thudding out of the trees, plus anacondas which are just too big and ugly to sneak up on anyone sober, though they could eat them whole if they did. Aside from those I'd also heard of some biting snakes, a local branch of pit vipers. And I knew that baby snakes carry venom, they're born fully loaded and ready to strike. I took a step or two back but this one didn't look perturbed. He lay like a special delivery.

Odds were pretty short that a snake could be found in this area. Also pretty short that a human would appear at this obvious threshold of a human dwelling with a doormat. But behind all this were long odds, is the thing. The odds attaching to the snake alone were the least of it. That background jungle of odds, the unbroken stream of it – never mind the horse race, what are the odds you even made it to the track? – in this case, due to the cascade of risk and chance down which I had surfed into a house on a hillside on an island where some dangerous snakes did roam – the odds were very long. The outcome of my presence on this doorstep was a feat of chance and serial influence.

And the snake will have taken its chances too.

Now here's the MacGuffin: it also happened that I had surfed onto a hillside in a place not only with snakes but a national lottery game that used mystical symbols alongside its thirty-six numbers. And *Little Snake* was the symbol for number twenty-seven. It also stood for a road and for the left wrist.

Following a friend's advice after I told him about the snake, I went out and put ten dollars on Little Snake. And it won that night's draw.

Not to suggest it was anything but a random lucky break, but I want to suggest we look at why I wouldn't suggest that, and to find out if I'm wrong. I want to look at our perception of risk and chance and see if it conforms to what we sense and see unfold. Maths and psychology platitude-laws like *probability* and *confirmation bias* are no longer a good enough plaster over this whole writhing world of odds. We need to rip that plaster off. Anyway the greatest example of confirmation bias is finding confirmation bias everywhere. No, no, we need to look at all this from scratch. It's time to look again. Stay with me as we ask: can we tune in to chaos and therefore influence chance?

Meanwhile Chaguanas

Chaguanas is a thriving town that grew out of a sugar estate beside a twelve-thousand-acre mangrove swamp. Caroni Swamp has neon scarlet ibises that make flamingos look bleached. From there they fly to Venezuela every day to feed and come back at night like red blood cells to pose around wetlands where four-eyed fish swim, overwatched by boas in trees. This is what we're talking about. The town itself is buzzing with food and tangled with overhead wires. Sited not too far north of the Hindu temple at Carapichaima, with its eighty-five-foot-tall Lord Hanuman statue, and some way south of Port of Spain, a highway drive away, commuting distance. This is where I'm going with Rebel this evening. We just said 'let's go'. The short film with the parrot is still unmade but forces are gathering towards it.

Meanwhile Chaguanas.

Rebel walked significantly taller and looked more chilled than his actual height and disposition would suggest. A hard man in a hot grimy world with the voice of a child actor. There was a rumour of music at a place under the tangled wires and Rebel said it would be a cultural highlight I would not want to miss. A cultural highlight of this rainbow island. I played Barrington Levy down the hill and we sailed out of town in fat evening air and saw the lights and signs after a while of Chaguanas. Smoking till we fizzed, it was that kind of night, with silicone air. When the venue appeared it was small, the kind of place on the kind of street where you'd put a fast-food joint. We entered a room under white strip lighting, bare as if awaiting better smells. Five young men and one girl of identical height, Rebel's height – compact – and identical clothing – black – were thrashing a pair of concert speakers with their waist-length black hair. The speakers were blasting out 'Torn From the Womb', by Autopsy. The cultural highlight.

'So – yeah,' said Rebel.

We stood and watched like parents.

Rebel chuckled and nodded as if to say that his country wasn't all steel drums. He broke into a grin at the pure lusty bang of thrashing your head to 'Torn From the Womb'. Just over the Madame Espagnol River from here tree boas were rustling or not rustling, four-eyed fish were pricking panes of black water, scarlet ibises were shot through the mangroves like moments after a murder against a hedge. And eleven or so miles beyond all of this, not far at all, the frothy edges of Venezuela bristled with swamps and songs and stories of their own, plus the long, long tail of Chávez. But here, just here – this was a place to thrash your hair.

We're just frozen at the doorway. There are no gradients between the still of night and Chris Reifert growling. I can only nod. We nod together. Nod and then lightly thrash. Grin. We grin together under the strip lights over a reflective tiled floor as a short distance away boas are rustling eleven or so miles from the long tail of Chávez; and something is correct about it, something's perfect, something's here that gets forgotten in fiction because fiction would go with the ibises or the death metal but would rarely go with both. We forget something important in the places we come from, if they're clean, cold affluent places where listlessness is a feature of childhood: we forget that the maths of risk and chance that leads to a plantation by a swamp producing kids to thrash their hair as boas hang in trees and four-eyed fish look on, is a lively maths. The boas and the swamp by themselves are a vigorous outcome. The whole gulf is a sprightly outcome, and the long tail of Chávez is a maths on its own. Evolution has here spent many more numbers than usual.

If nature is maths this is vivid maths.

More sums, more equations, more algorithms, more odds are here. The evidence is in front of our eyes. There's a lightbulb lizard here in the hills with reflectors built into its body. That is some mutation of natural maths. Is it not fair to ask Little Snake whether *our* outcomes are different here, are maths and physics different? If not directly, are we made different in our apprehension and comprehension, in our sense of them? Are the background odds more abundant in a place so bursting with vivid maths?

And Little Snake replies: why do you think the place has a daily numbers game where the numbers are indexed to symbols? Players under the influence of vivid maths need more than cold hard numbers: they need a channel for their dreams and superstitions, for omens and whims:

1. Centipede
2. Old Lady
3. Carriage
4. Dead Man
5. Parson Man
6. Belly
7. Hog
8. Tiger
9. Cattle
10. Monkey
11. Corbeau
12. King
13. Crapaud
14. Money
15. Sick Woman
16. Jammette
17. Pigeon
18. Water Boat
19. Horse
20. Dog
21. Mouth
22. Rat
23. Big House
24. Queen
25. Morocoy
26. Fowl
27. Little Snake
28. Red Fish
29. Opium Man
30. House Cat
31. Parson's Wife

32. Shrimp
33. Spider
34. Blind Man
35. Big Snake
36. Donkey

And due to vivid maths, Little Snake continues, once we get past Level One, which is numbers, this is still only Level Two of the ancient game of Chinapoo, or Whe-Whe, or Play-Whe, as we call the public game, because Level Three attaches body parts to the mystical icons, thirty-six between the left ear and right foot, including ribs, wrists, breasts and thighs, in case your clues manifest through your body, which after all is a product of prime maths. So while you've been busy with Health & Safety and a culture of thoughts that says chaos is bad, while at best you've felt a metallic thrill playing lotteries of indifferent numbers and radical odds, we've splashed every day in zestful maths, because if the vastness of the surf isn't hard enough to ignore, the glow of phosphorescence surely is. Even Level Three was insufficient to fathom that swell, we went up to Level Four and had our symbols mingle in stories, just as numbers mingle in chaos to throw up life, and just as you and I mingled on the doormat to signal a chance:

1-16-29: Centipede, Jammette, Opium Man = *Drunk man with a jammette at a bar.*
2-17-30: Old Lady, Pigeon, House Cat = *Old lady living with young girl in a house.*
3-18-31: Carriage, Water Boat, Parson's Wife = *A funeral but the dead are missing.*

14-29-6: Money, Opium Man, Belly = *Drunk man wasting his money.*

32-11-24: Shrimp, Corbeau, Queen = *Society woman having an affair.*

30-9-22: House Cat, Cattle, Rat = *Rat and cat stealing food: meat and milk.*

35-14-27: Big Snake, Money, Little Snake = *Money in the road.*

Possibilities fly out in a starburst of maths showing patterns in the chaos around, tying life's symptoms to symbols and tying those symbols to numbers: *a woman crying pregnant from an older man, a girl child talking and laughing her head off, a horsewhip snake hiding in a hole, a shootout ending in death …*

Little Snake seems firm on one point: that we can agree or disagree with the idea of a variable colour and temperature in maths, whether or not they intensify outcomes – but the tools of chance described above are the tools of a culture aware and admitting that it lives in a place of vivid maths. And these are some of the tools we use to tap into it, Little Snake appears to add.

Your science has reduced life to metrics until you don't trust your instinct or even feel it anymore. You forget how much you've forgotten. You've buried it under a set of complications designed to obscure: you've called the drunk man a noble victim and his wasting of money a deeper universal malaise – when the man is simply drunk and wasting money.

I think Little Snake's point here is that our clinging as a culture to numbers on paper without meeting the eye of the snake has even defeated our handling of the numbers on paper. Because we snubbed our old friendship with real-world maths and tried to make it our cash-cow bitch.

Little Snake is also saying maths may manifest differently from place to place. An island might be so powerful and such a mathematical Eden that it changes the way people perceive their chances, if not alters their chances as well. Vivid maths begets vivid creatures and when we look at the argument we can agree that a higher biodiversity including manatees, ocelots and boas breeds more intensive maths by definition: mutations are greater, odds grow longer between them, and the only real question is which one came first, maths or diversity, to which the answer must be maths. So this bushier background maths must make a difference, its odds must lose some purity when extracted in single strands. Note that wherever life thrives above the average like this, wherever a place is thick with trees and creatures and layer upon layer of genetic strategies, in other words thriving with maths, there's also usually a rich human lore of magic. Life in general in places like this runs at such a high pitch of maths that perhaps that competition between creatures, probabilities and their sums is what we now call vivid maths.

An internal competition for survival which results in the lightbulb lizard and the channel-billed toucan thriving together, so high have the numbers been driven in the district they share. And perhaps that contest for odds sparks the lores of magic we use to try and sway it in our favour. The only other places with massive maths are vast cities with huge populations, hectic places whose built-maths is more of a badly designed clutter than a free-wheeling system; that is to say the places where natural maths is corrupt and diluted, as well as the places which are rich and where remedial science can be bought to correct or enhance unwanted luck.

But any science dealing with the correction or enhancement of natural outcomes – whether it be virology, genetics or plastic surgery – is itself an admission of the existence of vivid maths, and a pursuit of it. It acknowledges Vivid Maths as the maths of the possible. Science is less interested in the probable. It senses that things can be done which today aren't possible and it gambles with vivid maths just as freely as the gamer to try and do them.

To think that laws of probability could change across their field of operation would ordinarily be magical thinking, but my problem with probability as we receive it in human culture is that it plays over such a long sample field, it could be a whole life or many millions of lives. We may not even live long enough for that field to yield the conclusion supporting the law. It is to say: we may lose by betting on Little Snake for the rest of our lives, but that doesn't mean we'll lose this time or next time. The law as it governs that bet says that any of thirty-six outcomes are equally probable – but what happens here in the existential world of decoherent reality is that one of them ups and wins. Doesn't matter the odds they all had: one ends up winning. And there's as wide a gap between the odds for thirty-six numbers and a single number win as there is between the still of the night and the snack bar in Chaguanas. That gap between swirling laws and outcomes is the gap of a spark plug throwing a spark; and Little Snake tells us that we have grown obsessed with the plug and not the spark.

The spark.

I had stopped by the little neighbourhood shop near the

beer shop in Woodbrook. Quiet lady in an iron cage with cigarettes and snacks. I filled in the Play-Whe card and put ten dollars on Little Snake. We were now in a pact.

We can be clear: no randomised lottery game can be remotely influenced by a player finding a snake on a doorstep. This was a straight thirty-six to one bet and it came in. That's the science. Cold simple maths. Odds aren't even that long.

But finding a little snake on the day Little Snake is about to win:

those odds are fucking long.

The Probability Bacchanal

And then there are human-to-human probabilities. Potentially vivid but more often a clusterfuck. I was lying back in bed watching this bat fly circuits up high through the gaps between the walls and the roof. It had a pattern of appearing every few minutes from the direction of the bedroom next door. It would circle to my bathroom before disappearing the way it had come. I imagined it flew a patrol of all the rooms, presumably prowling for bugs. Waiting for this circuit was akin to counting sheep in slow motion. And this one time I remember I also lay reflecting on a local post-office worker in a passive-aggressive feud with me. That's what it was. I didn't start it. Type of shit that makes you sigh. Type of person who hasn't danced enough. Must be the only one on the island. Some anal vendetta on account of a package I had to collect from the office which they swore they had tried to deliver and onto which they then slapped an interest-breeding fee.

My position was that I wanted the fee waived because

they hadn't tried to deliver. I'd had to call them after the package didn't show up, knowing it had been sent. But what happens is that the treacherous eastern face of my street and driveway so enervates the postie that he'd rather retire without a pension than walk up the hill again. And I understand this. Thirty-two-degree heat. Mega humidity. It's okay. I can walk down. There's no mailbox outside the house so you have to come up and knock. The package wouldn't fit in a mailbox anyway. But now another person at the post office, presumably unaware of all the entropy surrounding my driveway, has taken umbrage at my resistance to paying the fine. This is one slice of that day's pie of odds, plus I still had the film to make with a parrot. It could only be a Tuesday. Fireflies flash outside the window which makes them look too busy for questions. But the bat might engage in passing.

Let's dissect this spat. We have three actors in three remote positions who are brought to intersection by the arrival of a package. Only one of them has the overview knowledge, presuming the postman doesn't bitch too much about Nemesis Hill to his colleagues. That overview knowledge only came to be needed because this one actor here, talking to the bat, is the one who has to pay the fine for 'all their trouble trying to deliver' the package. In fairness this person at the post office, who we'll just call Vendetta, may spend their life confronting arguments, in fact may even have been hired for the thickness of their skin in the face of arguments and resistance to fines. They may have attended workshops on pious lecturing and talk-to-the-hand behaviours. I don't know why a person is so quick to launch vendettas. The person may have been the middle child in a household where vendettas were a thing. And now we're tracing cascades back through

Vendetta's parents to a whole ancestral line, quintillions of cascades leading to this breaking edge of reality, dawn of humankind, where she's launching a vendetta on me. This is how she spends her cascades. As for the postie, he could have a long and accomplished history of scaling my driveway, in fact I've seen him do it. I've even hung over a walkway ledge to relieve him of his load before he reached the top. Odds weren't against him coming up at all, according to his past form.

Other broader odds could come to bear: perhaps morale at the post office took a turn for the worse. Some new boss could've broken the postie's spirit for scaling heights. A hopeless mood could be invading the office as ink slips through water in a glass. Just see the cascading odds: we have the odds of a street being an unappealing climb for the person whose job it is to climb it; we have the wider odds of being a talk-to-the-hand negotiator, in the case of the post-office worker, which are short odds and shortening every day; we have the odds of that actor being connected to the actor who won't climb the street, which are longer; and then we have the odds that destiny's switches and cogs would pick me as the actor between them in a mail hostage situation with a ransom.

My problem is that these kinds of averages are long dynamic chains that gush from birth and even earlier, all the way back to the odds of a planet developing life. Moreover on this side of birth all the odds are human-influenced, which blurs true chance with a thumb of intervention, and adds a universe more in terms of what we choose to do. And we three actors share this feature. The feature is a virtual infinity of interconnected probabilities stretching back to the dawn of time – and we're only three beings among billions of others with their own dice in play. The point is we *swim* through maths all our lives. Then when we feel like it we pick one filament of that colossal bagatelle in the form of a die or a horse or a pack of cards. In the form of a snake or a corbeau or a parson's wife. And science has the tools to call some odds for an outcome; but it only assesses the filament in isolation. And I ask how is that filament not connected to the hand that grasped it, to the sum, to the spirit and nature and force of the cascade that grew it?

We can't expect mathematicians to spend their lives working out how the AD 1700 invasion of Swedish Estonia connects to these chips I dropped on the floor. So they don't and probably can't. But those maths exist nonetheless and had fully material consequences. One of those sums put these chips on the floor. So we're facing a paradoxical task as we press ahead to explore all this: one is to be aware of that spinning vortex of sums and its power to manifest hard outcomes. The other is to ignore it for the purposes of calculation. We're going to look for another way into the space where maths decoheres into reality. A place where statistics can't help us, by which I mean the odds that say nearly half of us will experience mental illness in our lifetime, that one in seventeen of us will die from an injury and one in three won't get enough sleep – because here's the thing: *which fucking ones*? This approach to maths drives all our little fears these days, drives vast initiatives by governments imposing outrageous imaginary likelihoods, the existential truth of which mean *fucking nothing*.

Which ones of us will get it? Which ones?

For instance, we're led to believe certain truths about our life expectancy. Yet by adjusting for infant mortality, life expectancy for my equivalent in ancient Greece before the time of Christ was as good or better than for me in the decade I was born. Life expectancy in mid-Victorian times was pretty much what it is today. The difference in the numbers once you account for infant deaths can be forty years. Yet we're still encouraged to imagine a world before the advent of cook-ie-dough ice cream where adults all died at thirty. Add to this that nearly half of ancient Greeks didn't suffer mental illness. Nearly half of mid-Victorians didn't suffer mental illness.

That our numbers are different is less disconcerting than triumphs or dangers being fed via statistics meant to change our perceptions of risk for a third party's benefit, or worse, to support a vague fiction of progress. Those same tools of thought also call odds on gambling and they suffer from the same problem: the sample is a count of dead events across too long and too corruptible a static span of time. And only the negatives are presented. If half of us will fall mentally ill it also means billions of us won't. So if two of us stand together the chances for all intents and purposes are equally split between neither of us will, both of us will, and one or the other of us will. And when will this lottery be drawn so we can know who will? Only when one of us falls mentally ill or both of us die. That's how long the span is. It tells us nothing about today, and today could bring the chance that cuts our risk by half, which kills the model.

What we seek in this inquiry is the home of the spark that decides *which one* of us will win. *Which outcome* is the next to be born here.

One last kick at the numbers on our way out the door: Harvard statistics graduate Persi Diaconis has proven that even coin tosses aren't a fifty-fifty chance. If a coin launches on heads it will mostly fall on heads. He was able to train himself to get it ten times out of ten. This is also why we inquire. Why we put aside the numbers and instead see if Little Snake is a way into the clearing where outcomes are born. We need to remember the curious number of hostage-situation survivors who knew before a shot was fired who among them would die.

A knowing. Something like a tunnel through the odds.

At the time of the postal vendetta I was as enervated to calculate the odds of the situation as the postie was to climb up to the place. I just went and paid the damn fine at the post office. Vendetta was still sour about it.

Two weeks later I heard of another package on its way.

The Unfairness of
Postal Work

Those redoubtable postal workers. Probably stymied by shifting conditions and low morale. Cut off from the charms of vivid maths by the spell-quashing grind of routine. And stuck now wrangling this chance-cascade that sent a package to some fucker up an alp. But look at this: vendettas aside, those tireless actors of chance also throw a light on one good reason to gamble, a reason many can feel but few ever talk about: *the unfairness of civilisation.*

Civilisation is also unfair because Chance is not fresh and pure in it. No longer organic. Few of life's chances are randomised in civilisation because they have somebody's fingerprint on them, distorting the beam of true odds. Since antiquity the Chinese have made an ardent tradition of mitigating this by appealing directly to luck. And can so many be wrong? Strictly speaking they can, but what we're out to see on our adventure with Little Snake is if true right or wrong can even exist in the face of cascading maths and the correctness of every moment.

If there exists a mathematical wheel of Fortuna with a set of universal odds then it must largely decohere when it hits civilisation; that is, the greatest number of seemingly random outcomes will be reactions to actions to reactions to actions that started with a human will. Odds aren't so much distorted as erased and replaced by behavioural odds like swarming wasps of kismet, and we're not talking about obvious corruptions such as national lotteries printing rollover posters before the draw rolls over, we're talking about a serendipitous three-dimensional mesh of interactivity from which no one can detach themselves.

There are as many stories in civilisation as there are atoms in the universe. Just picture one of them: you grow an abiding love of cardboard by your fifth birthday, along with a precocious expertise in rubber stamps. Your aunts encourage your genius with gifts of a stapler and tape, and by your twelfth birthday you have a job wrapping gift-boxes for a distance-seller down the road. You graduate from high school and you're soon snapped up by the second most important name in pet haircare products where you spend five of your best years advancing pet haircare product packaging. And when the chief packager's corner office becomes vacant, with the window and the spider plant, you're the obvious choice by a mile. Your calling has primed you for this. You poise to ascend.

Then that fucker Brian gets the job because he drinks with the boss. You quit and wind up working at an island post office.

This is the milieu of civilisation.

The pure fresh odds called in by your energies across the years of your vocation met Brian. They converted into Brian's odds. Most odds in civilisation are second-hand odds, volleyed and spun by human actors or by conditions caused by their actions. Nothing true about those odds. If we want true odds we have to skip civilisation and gamble. Not on horses or dogs, which can also be rigged, not even card games where deception is a skill; no, no, to access raw code in the universe it takes coins, dice and roulette wheels. Bets on raindrops.

On raw newly-minted maths, clear as a trout stream.

This must also be why we gamble. And why wouldn't we? Feel that cool steely stream around our fingers. Gambling is how we leave town and drive up to that crystalline idyll of maths. And if the unfairness of civilisation is something we're aware of but don't talk about as a model of odds, and if we're aware on some level of our own participation in it, then we're aware of its negative weight, and we spend our lives aware. Asphyxiated by civilisation, of course we're going to clutch at pure maths. The asphyxia of unfairness causes it. And some of us dull the frustration with booze and destruction, a slow risk-cascade – or else we reach into the ether to touch the source.

Since the fucking corner office was meant to be ours.

Duck Curry

Shocks of flame swallowed forms in the cane fields. We passed like the damned looking into hell but seeing it as paradise, with wiry figures shimmering through heat, bending and bowing in the crops rolling by, just as the first indentured East Indians must have done when they landed on this island with their proud beautiful names like Moonsammy. The heat of it blasted through open car windows. My guests slouched around like dropped towels as this maths of flames and names rolled by. This chapter's road trip was funded by winnings from Little Snake. I'm blowing them on two friends who flew in from Paris, a surfing chef and a male underwear model who also proposes to surf, using some of the time I might have spent on a short commercial film with a parrot. Parrots are easier said than done so instead we cruise through the cane fields of central Trinidad on our way to a shack among cashews and mangos where new friends of mine have killed a duck to make a curry. The main friend is from indentured stock himself, now in a land of milk and honey. It was some risk those first arrivals took, contracts of up to ten years before they could sail home to Calcutta, back when boats were wooden and life was salty. In the end most of them never went back, they stayed to add to the island's soul, to spread their blazing culture, and it was a roll of the dice. But they came with their gods and good practices. Milk and honey out here in the cane fields, unless you wanted the townhouse in Manhattan. These friends don't want the townhouse as they're happy out here with their chickens and ducks, just one of those places where the roosters never stop crowing but where it's good in the same way that crickets are the music of dreams.

Granted I don't live with the roosters.

I wonder if their forebears had enough information to imagine the land they were coming to. I wonder how much their expectations influenced what happened to them, although they paid in sweat for everything they got. But building upwards over a length of time calls for deliberate good practices in working with luck. We call those practices 'growing up' when really they're conditionings flowing from good and bad outcomes in our management of opportunity, which some people never get right. The conscious mind can overcomplicate things and distort our perceptions of chance, which in turn can mess things up.

We can also influence ourselves with confidence or self-disturb with fear which may alter the climate around us in a physical way, as well as transmit those signals to others. Perhaps it can. And if our chemistry, our magnetism, have waveforms like light and sound, they may affect nearby maths just as plants are affected by music. With this in mind, how much does our thinking about particular outcomes put those outcomes into play?

That it might influence numbers is magical thinking, but over a beer along the road to this shack with the duck, it's much more fun than maths. And it is still mathematical. Little Snake set me thinking differently about chaos and risk. I'm not a mathematician so it's not to say my original position on how the universe works was any good. But if the material world is defined by hard maths then our mythology can only be too. Everything can only be – yet still we focus on the material object, not on its ideas, its climate and symbols. Its moment. The moment it collapses from chance into finality. Ignoring this dimensional environment of chance seems more of a modern western phenomenon, and maybe it accounts for the shabby image gambling ended up with. Even the word itself is heavily shop-soiled.

Cast your mind back to your first impressions of gambling: it was sold to us as a numbers racket, a criminal enterprise by criminals for other criminals. Our first impression of gambling comes pre-loaded with the idea that it's unwise. A world prevails of film-star gangsters, losers, losing statistics and down-and-out tropes. But then came Little Snake. Little Snake attached our gambling to humanity and metaphysics and with that somehow to life. It gave a sense that *winning wasn't the sole objective*. That in placing the Little Snake bet we were signposting our love of unfolding life and feeding it back via maths to the source of the cascade that brought the snake. A feedback loop with the universe. It sounds religious and it is religious. Little Snake is at once an omen, a prompt to live life and a heat-exchange with God.

It just cannot be right that we swim through cascades of

everyday neutral chances and then the maths attached to a gamble automatically falls into hopelessness, even when the odds are rigged in the house's favour. There cannot be two sets of maths according to whether we're being sensible or foolish. But this is how it's presented: if we engage in foolish cascades of chance to marry and build a family it's noble and those odds are neutral, though we all know we can still wind up wretched – but if we gamble we've gone straight to hell.

And for sure that smutty pall comes from all the cash that's involved. It's the amount invested and lost that counts to us, and that smut spreads over the maths of gambling itself because *losers often seem to keep losing*. That losers so commonly keep losing suggests an influence over the outcome of the game, especially considering that odds at a casino blackjack table may only lean 0.5 per cent in the house's favour. We can lose via reckless strategy of course, as in the amounts we wager and when; but does that mean losers are trying to lose? I doubt it.

This is the thing. We're looking at a birthspace between the maths and the outcome, and it must be influenced by, and connected to, the cascades around and before it. That notional climate of non-stop cascades is our personal aura, like a circulatory system of a breeze as alive and bewitching as the silent furry bat that circulates above my head in a tropical house on a tropical island; and surely that's where we must focus our religion.

We turn left through a gap in a cane field and after a while bounce on dirt up a hill to a shack with an oil drum full of cool water watched over by a hammock between poles on a porch. It's the place. It's midday and it's hot. A pot of yellow-green curry boils away on a fire by the entrance while luckier ducks traipse around between trees dotting off into bushland with bright red phalli hiding single cashew nuts. The friends, a married couple, are lit up. The curry is bright, the rum is strong, we eat and joke and dip in the drum of water. Vividly.

I guess what we're trying to say is that we forget the universality of maths. We take one minuscule strand which is a wager on the immediate future while around us cascades of tumbling chance equal all the particles in the universe times its age times fifty trillion. We pick one tiny thing and go Yay or Oops. Watching these ducks for instance: one was unlucky to go into the pot. But we were lucky it went in. The same chance manifested positive and negative. The event-cascade coiling down to the duck's death will be a cable of many twines. These friends must pick their ducks according to something, it wouldn't all be luck, but then maybe it would, who knows if one duck is like another, if the couple develops early knowledge of which is for the pot, if one's their least favourite, or if they wanted the biggest and fattest for this curry; or perhaps they just grabbed the closest one, maybe they lunged, it fled, and they got the next fastest.

Little Snake reminds us that the amount of natural lotteries the duck had to live through to reach the pot, from the primal lottery of being born a duck and not a snake, are almost infinite. In the end the duck was born slow or unlucky by that day's odds. It was our friends' most or least favourite, or the fattest, or the one that just looked at them the wrong way on that softly sweltering day with flames and forms and shimmering smoke in the cane fields. These are mere fractions of the algorithm of winning, duck-wise, on that one day. And the duck didn't see it coming till it was too late. We can't know what we don't observe and the universe doesn't want us to observe everything. Albert Einstein once said: 'Nature hides her secrets because of her essential loftiness, but not by means of ruse.' That truth manifests here even for ducks.

As we've bumped into Einstein we should pause and take stock of how our snake-infested vivid ideas sit with actual science and maths, since for me they sit very close. It was also Einstein who said: 'As far as the laws of mathematics refer to reality, they are not certain; and as far as they are certain, they do not refer to reality.' He also said: 'Mathematics are well and good but nature keeps dragging us around by the nose.' Einstein's ideas on the universe, still widely accepted by physicists, proposed a single, pliable, four-dimensional space we call the 'block universe'. And everything in Einstein's universe, including the nature of the future, was decided at the outset and is set for ever. This must be why our current way of thinking imagines that everything is technically predictable.

For instance, it's possible in Einstein's universe to forecast the weather to an exact degree; we just don't have the tools to measure every single puff of wind and raindrop on the planet. So our sciences today, and especially technology, push ahead trying to build more intimate tools based on a line of thought that pretty much singlehandedly created the world we're bitching about. But here's the crucial thing: while a majority of physicists still abide by the notion of a block universe, because it's predicted by general relativity – others pondering beyond it have grown less sure of its implications. And that may be due to the same screaming gap that underpins our torrid inquiry: since despite our overwhelming sense of surfing a present reality into a wide open future, *nowhere in physics is the present accounted for – and the future is already fixed*. All we can do is discover what it's fixed to do. Einstein wrote not long before his death: 'The distinction between past, present and future is only a stubbornly persistent illusion.' But you and I are moving parts in this same universe, block or otherwise, extremely rare and vibrant agents, and our lived experience is of cascades that break like waves into past realities. We actually *discover* reality as it breaks around us. Classical physics has done no less than conveniently write out of existence the majority experience of the creature which invented classical physics – and has moreover declared us delusional. This is what the fuck we're really facing. And we're not the first to question this chasm between science and lived reality, just the first with this duck in a curry. Some, like Swiss physicist Nicolas Gisin, have pointed a finger at inadequate maths. In Gisin's case he recently turned to a century-old mathematical language called *intuitionist mathematics*, which states that maths is a product of the human mind and not a discovery of existing objective principles. It rejects the idea of numbers with infinitely many digits, and reimagining physical systems this way led Gisin to find that 'Time really passes and new information is created.' Later in the course of our rampage we'll also look at Einstein's bête noire, the quantum physicists whose entire business is breaking reality.

Meanwhile Einstein can put us back with the ducks and curry: 'Imagination is more important than knowledge,' he said, and what we're imagining here is that, not only as moving parts in a universal mathematical system but as creators of it, we know what's going on without the damn numbers.

What if the long cascade of chances travelling through apes and ancestors grew so familiar to us that we've allowed or even driven ourselves to ignore it? That we've stylised life's dynamics to an extent where the primal cascade of chance is seen as an unfashionable and primitive thought. By cumulative boredom over millions of years or by our growing acumen or ignorance or outright terror at simply being alive, we grew obsessed with the metrics and buried the senses that feel the mathematical engine of natural things. What if we were so a part of the chance-cascade, so of its flesh that we stopped looking outwards?

And what if gambling is our finger back in that socket? Gambling with life, gambling with games and gambling with thoughts in the mind. Maths giveth and maths taketh away unless you play with cheats, but even their existence still comes under the governance of maths. Gambling: a finger into the current to see if it gives or takes. To see if we are *favoured*. If we are *lucky*. If we are *alive*.

What if gambling is a braille of nature? A code to calibrate our links to chaos, a language of larger life. As we do seem to like that crackling socket of reality, and not just for games: much of life in society is a pinball of gambles.

Napoleon said great events always hang by a hair, and they do seem to, which also asks if there's a policy of brinkmanship in chance, if not in chaos itself. Black and white are built into our thinking on chance, or else we would have devised a gaming token that didn't win or lose but left us equal. Instead we bet the house which makes you wonder if absolutes are nature's favoured chauffeurs.

The sun is yellow and lower on the hill behind the cane fields. Clouds roil over the Northern Range which is the forested tailbone of the Andes chopped off at Venezuela. Violent vivid maths along these coasts and we're dozing on the porch amid the spent cascades of the day, a tickertape of maths in scented breezes. Around us the speeding cables of live cascades on their way from the dawn of time to the end, maths beyond lightspeed on its way to the future. The wake of that stream froths around us in rum, cane smoke, cashews and ducks.

Trinidadians on this hill whose forebears embarked from hometowns in India will know something about chance. It's been said that some were outright tricked into coming by agents earning a bounty for each labourer. Two hundred and twenty-seven souls came on the first boat out of Calcutta but many more stayed behind. The ones who stayed were lucky as they weren't tricked. The ones who were tricked were unlucky to be tricked but later inherited a paradise. Among those who stayed and those who came, some will be luckier than others.

The sun trembles through this cane smoke as it would through running water and we leave our friends behind with their chickens and ducks. I ruminate that the duck was lucky to roam on this hill and we were lucky to eat it. Its eventual bad luck and our good luck came as an all-or-nothing chance. Life is this way and a toss of one coin bears as much chaos-nature as that. It must be of the same maths stream. Driving north over dirt to meet the road back into town I can't say if I remember that our road trip was floated by Little Snake. I can't say if I remember that twenty-seven, Little Snake, also stands for a road. But I remember it today and nod my head – Little Snake put us out on this road.

Renting the Parrot

Behind that time behind the cane fields there was this film to make with a parrot. A parrot is a tropical trope and I believe in both tropics and tropes. Of course a short tropical film was going to have a parrot, what else would it have. Parrots live in tropics. A lot of my fiction plays with tropes: well-fitting, ill-fitting and florid tropes, because despite proclaiming our uniqueness we invariably add up to a curated shorthand of clues, as seen by others; and since the characters in a fiction are others, and tropes are a root of human frailty and discord, they should be a root of human fiction too, why not? Moreover we use tropes by default: starting in childhood when scamming a day off school means adopting the manner of a gravely ill person. Plus tropes offer a snap-to-grid function for media. The Blue-Collar Gandhi. The Child Society Failed. The Once-Illustrious Loser. And thus for us via that influence, becoming a snap-to-grid for our narratives of ourselves and others. Even arguing our uniqueness is a trope.

Thus the tropics needed a parrot. This was my mistake with the maths of tropes. By now some way into the project's development I wanted the damn thing to talk as well. My colleagues and I put out the word across the island for the right kind of bird, which couldn't be that hard to find, you would think, in a place with boas and toucans. We didn't even need an extravagant bird, and the talking was still fairly optional – but weeks went by without a hint of a parrot at all.

Then eventually came news of a quiet boy on the far coast with a bird that fit the bill. We called to make an offer, sitting up like fishermen to a bite – but despite the fixer's best efforts the boy didn't sound too keen. He said the boy was in an other-worldly parrot romance, that his bond with the bird was more sublime than any human bond, which was wonderful news to us and a trope in itself. The fixer added that it mainly translated into high-price expectations. We invited the boy up to talk it over, and he came to Port of Spain with his bird. It had a yellow crown on a cool green body and could talk a little. We didn't really need it to speak but just open its beak so we could dub a voice in later. It could do this.

We had decided we would shoot our little project on celluloid, hence we called it a film. An old-school movie, a larger-than-life production, a parrot Shangri-La which we would shoot on a wild, empty beach, surely that wouldn't be hard to find on the island. As we explained this to the boy and described the sweep of the beach with our hands, looking up towards the ceiling as if the dream would there appear, he seemed to soften and grow more interested in the fee we would pay for the bird. We assured him of an active role in the shoot, as a fully retained parrot wrangler, and he agreed, telling us the bird would only perform for him anyway.

Our budget was limited but the parrot would naturally be paid in line with industry standards and more. It would have a sunflower-seed and mineral-water rider. Wrangler and bird would be fed, transported and cared for. By now we knew that odds for sourcing a parrot were long, and the boy in his quietness was soaking up the office-scape, carpeted as it was and air-conditioned to Arctic standards. Even before we explained that there would be two separate shoots – one for blue-screen shots in a studio, one on location at the beach – he absorbed our surroundings and the fee went up in his mind. Through a doorway he could also see and hear the accountant keying maths into a machine. She was glamorous, sharp and formidable, and the ring of her clacking machine foretold a fortune to come. We watched it happen, even the parrot cocked its head.

The parrot got expensive. Here's what had happened: I had calculated much shorter odds of finding a bird. Shorter odds would have made their market weaker. As it happened odds were long and their market was strong. And here's the rub: I hadn't known the odds and neither had the boy. For all he knew we had a casting session that afternoon with a hundred more parrots who could recite whole scripts. But we didn't have a casting session and he gathered that truth when we were hesitant to bluff that we did. As a coastal boy unconnected to us in any way he also didn't buy into the idea that we were usually this attentive to parrots.

This is how true odds are assessed when they come second hand through people. Odds and prices are set without a word needing to be spoken. Setting odds, parrying risks and bluffing prices are the human arts of converting cascades of chance belonging to others. This is how we've developed in the face of cascading maths. See how adept we've become. We should look at this more closely.

In the meantime we hired the parrot.

Quantum Reprise

Do our thoughts outside the body have mass? Does our energy? Is there a space between the spark of probability and its outcome for a bolt of ours to influence chance? What of the inner force we use to influence dogs? Granted: the dog is also living and keen to follow clues. But still that energy is transmitted: where else can it transmit? Where else does it transmit?

Some hours later the drinks wear off and this is revealed to be magical.

But what if the magic is real?

Ah!

Soul Gambling

What about these human arts then? prompted Little Snake, who had rendered them futile by the power of snake arts. And well, we could say that gambling is such a human thing that it rewards both winners and losers, in that some of us seek out negative affirmation, on which we sometimes also thrive.

The man who put me on the highway to winning purposefully was called Roberto: a Vietnam veteran who, after turning me onto salsa legend Ismael Rivera, brought on my backgammon skills in record time by playing for cash from the outset and beating the shit out of me. He did this with a crocodile smile and a husky chuckle which made him exactly who you would cast as the Jungian mentor-trickster in a movie. It was an invitation to compete. Whether or not he won individual games of backgammon, which I could already play, he caned me overall using betting strategy with the lethal doubling cube. In case you're unfamiliar with the doubling cube in backgammon it's the larger die with Arabic numerals that sits in the game-set with the dice. It's not menacing until you lose money to it, then it commands respect followed by angst followed by fear followed by terror. How it works is that at a certain point in the game the doubling cube is offered by one player to another to increase the bet. If you refuse the cube you default the game, but if you accept it the cube moves into your possession. You can then offer it back, but here's the sting: the stakes don't rise in sequential digits, they go two, four, eight, sixteen, thirty-two, sixty-four, and that number multiplies the original stake. The cube can get to sixty-four before the game is half over. When it does, you just go round again, two is one hundred and twenty-eight, four is two hundred and fifty-six, and so on. If the game was for a friendly bet of ten bills the thing is now two thousand five hundred and sixty and climbing for as long as anyone can do the maths. That cube can pass back and forth until you're in deep financial peril and the game becomes a test of who can even concentrate, let alone keep their nerve.

Desperation is not favourable for gambling. Gambling at its heart is funded by desperate people for sanguine people. So this was Roberto's wise approach and he'd chuckle and we'd smoke and guzzle icy rum in the upstairs wooden office of his rambling wooden building beside a levee in sultry Texas. Where I quickly and expensively learned how to win and lose at backgammon.

Within a year I was tramping up broad red-carpeted stairs to an uppermost innermost members-only club devoted to backgammon. This was before Little Snake, back home in Mexico City where backgammon was always the rage. I don't like members-only places but I was a member. The drinks were still pricy but that wasn't the point. I now know the point was a vivid maths environment. A setting for the generation of amps between people and dice. Dark, dark, smoky, air-conditioned air and tight, tight spotlights. The wind-chime tune of bold, polished ice cubes in glass. A powdery thud of chips on leather. And gambling. Gambling was banned at the club and there was a sign to this effect which we all knew meant that gambling was revered and applauded but don't exchange monetary instruments here in the bar or we will fall foul of our licence. This made the games even juicier. Honour was involved as our wagers couldn't even be scribbled down in plain sight. Settlement at some other location was discreetly agreed, which was often in the bathroom as you were already there on young business. But it could be anywhere, honour was key. There was even credit and lending.

This was a million miles from sultry Texas but I kept the Texan swelter fondly to heart because here in a place among over-shined shoes and impeccable cuffs I had the tools to make people shit themselves. I may not have been any better player but I had seen what the cube could do. I didn't know the maths but I thought I could feel it, I played with my gut alone. This can also disturb mathematical players as what they think are errors can lead to a win.

What I learned from backgammon apart from romancing the dice – which I always lobbied to hold in my hand and not in a dice-cup – was the division of gambling forces into two distinct strands, two beams, one being its own chances relayed through the dice and the other being my chances against an opponent's. Neither of us could in theory influence chance travelling through the dice, though I felt I could do it with tequila – but we could influence each other's state of mind. There had been a time early on when I played with types who would start a game declaring they would win. This irritated me because they were using the seed of that thought as a weapon, and once it's planted it grows and grows. I hadn't known how to counter it except with the same ammunition of bravado, flat-out replying that I would win first, but it just seemed too late and too lame. It wasn't until Texas that I found the higher tool of the doubling cube, which worked on two levels: it acted more powerfully on an opponent's mind than telling them I would win; it also made an opponent's declaration, if they'd made it, look like a desperate empty bluff. It was the highest ground of the ruthless board.

That cube makes players its bitch.

Then you just have to win.

The Weather is Coral Snakes

Winning comes in as many forms as there are moments in reality. For road-trip excursions in Trinidad such as the ones we'd take to shoot this film with the parrot, I had a big unfashionable four-door car with air conditioning and a cassette player. This was a win. Roughly the third cassette that had gone in the player was *Night of the Wolverine* by Dave Graney and the Coral Snakes. But it got stuck in the player and became the only soundtrack for the rest of the year. More snakes. It was an auto-reverse cassette player, way out of date but cool, clunky and tactile, with a sound you'd get from good wooden speakers – and it just kept flipping over and repeating. Now, I'm into Dave Graney, this was no hardship. But anyone who rode in this car more than once thought I lived in a Dave Graney universe, and I did, except it was really a travelling microclimate. *Night of the Wolverine* could be heard from top to bottom of the island. I was the driver and it rained Dave Graney.

Then an office runner got the tape out by magic one day. He got it out by not knowing it was stuck fast, by just expecting it to pop out, that's the energy he used. It took him extra effort but a knack came to him, I think with help from his keys, and – *click*. Later we must explore this fertile area of chance, the luck that seems to spring from simply not computing the risk.

This office runner was an affable guy, his grin was literally attached to his ears, and when he saw you from his errand bike in his helmet all you could see was that grin. It was unusual to have him in the car, though he was welcome; but this day he had burning issues on his mind. He had partner trouble, issues of high incendiary passion which he still used his gentle voice to express. His partner wasn't doing what he wanted, apparently, wasn't dressing the way he wanted, in other words was failing to do what he thought was the right thing, the expected thing. I didn't know who his partner was. My colleague who was gentle and known for his grin had also downloaded this culture of ideas and had notions about how things should be. As I tried a route into the question I sensed it was going to be a long job. In the midst of it all he wanted to play me his personal mix tape to vent some passions, and in the midst of that, without even really thinking about it, he used the power of love-trouble-miracles to flip the Dave Graney tape out of the player. I watched it happen before my eyes. He went at it with fresh, purposeful, innocent energy. Calm assertive energy, as we say.

His mix tape kicked off with 'Bitches Ain't Shit' and the job of romantic counselling grew even longer. I never put

Dave Graney and the Coral Snakes back into the deck after that, in case it got terminally stuck. Years later when I gave up being a parrot scout to write about this parrot instead, Dave Graney wrote to me out of the blue. I told him I had spent a year with *Night of the Wolverine*.

The odds of this particular cascade are much much longer than any gamble, probably even a lottery. These are our starting points for the flow of odds: unique and never to be repeated in the history of the universe – and only then do Dave Graney's odds come in. As if, depending on where you cut off the sample, there may be no short odds for anything in existence. Our tuning of odds towards an average may be skewed if we treat every chance as born anew today. But in this there's another question: the cascade that led to this story started long before I arrived in Trinidad, it was a chain of many links – would the nature of a gamble be the same if we bet on one link as if we bet on the whole cascade?

Courting Uncertainty

Not to overcomplicate this but we need to add a factor to our world of chance-cascades. We've been talking about the length of them, whole chains of events versus single events by themselves, and about gauging longer sections of chain to judge risk and assess the polarity of chance, find the positive and negative. But Little Snake prompts me that there's another factor to consider which is *adjacent cascades*.

What happens when cascades run together? Our favourite bar in parrot times stood under a cliff behind Port of Spain, in a neighbourhood aptly called Cascade. Parrot season also saw the bar's genial host tragically killed flying back from a cricket match in a light aircraft that crashed into the sea off St Vincent. But at the start of evening drinks one random Friday when he was still around, as the crowd was lighting up on beer and rum, I suddenly started to feel like shit. I bailed out early for the first time in memory and drove up the hill to bed. Next day I awoke feeling worse and decided to go out and find a doctor.

I had seen a small sign near the corner of a residential street in town, with a fine East Indian name and a promise of medicine, and I drove around until I saw it again. It was a private house and the doctor happened to be there. He ushered me to a battered armchair that could have been used by earlier generations watching cricket and football in his little sitting room, while he took a seat in a bureaucrat's old swivel chair. He was quiet and clear and observed me like a real doctor, that is, like a doctor with time to let a patient's conversation wash over them before judging their state.

After a brief examination he looked at me and said: 'You're suffering from two unconnected things.' Now this could be a routine diagnostic outcome in medicine, I don't know, but I was impressed. Two things. Unconnected. Two cascades, adjacent, and within ten minutes he not only knew this but knew what they were: a tropical virus plus a parasite. He wrote out a prescription and I was fine within a day or two. Best medic ever. But thinking about it now those two chance clinical occurrences, the result of their own cascades, had caused one big malaise. Each would have caused sickness but they got together by chance and caused a bigger one. The lesson must be that cascades together can flow into single outcomes and potentiate them. And if it happens by chance, maybe it can happen by design; I say it as there had also been a time when I instinctively tried to join cascades into one for a single bet on a horse race, marshalling them together like a cable of multiple twines. I was after bigger advantage, but also trying to hedge against the sting of lone gambles and lost love.

This was the season that came after backgammon, when I would walk down a disused railway cutting to a betting shop. Crunchy gritted trail. Different country altogether, in fact a distinct enough life from the one before that it felt like a reincarnation. I had known this betting shop was there but until this particular season of life it had held as much interest as a dry cleaner's. I was not a big gambler, game-wise. I am not a big gambler today. But that was a season of gambles upon gambles upon gambles. I had opened the spigot of chance to full bore and now had to figure it out. So I steamed down this cutting for about a mile.

Railway tracks were gone, trains were gone, the empty cutting ran like an open roofless tunnel behind a neighbour-hood, rising to level ground and falling under again. It was both a trench and a path that looked like you should walk down it, and I did, at speed and bent forward as if against a wind. The social security office was the busiest building in this area that was clotted like calcium to the artery of a broad outskirts avenue strewn with low-rent businesses and drive-thru fast food. I liked the place. Behind this artery lay an outer suburb of uncoiled hoses, porches on bungalows and the sound of mowing on weekends. A real place with wind and vandalism and the menace of vicious nesting birds that would swoop down and attack you, a place of abandoned toys, barbecue smoke and expletives; there's one in every town that lies on flat ground.

Almost no foot traffic at all around there, except to reach twelve-year-old cars. I was the foot traffic and I barrelled down this cutting every day, eventually turning down one of the shadier streets where things were less trimmed to emerge back on the highway at this betting shop. Not a big shop, twelve to fifteen people would be a crowd there, it was a glass-fronted locale in a row of glass-fronted locales more suited to fried chicken. A woman and a man with smoky down-to-earth faces and arid wit would work the counter behind a glass partition. After a couple of visits they got used to you and became friendly, once you'd picked up the rhythm and vernacular of the place, which you did by watching regulars craning up at the screens and snarling 'Mongrel!' It may not have even been the gambling that first drew me in, as there was a bureaucracy to betting-shop gambling which I knew little about. Rather I must have been sucked to the door by the treasure of discarded cigarettes in the ashtray outside, being so poor at the time that I wasn't above lighting dog-ends. The betting shop was gold for dog-ends as smoking was banned indoors and punters had to come out to soothe their nerves, grow their courage and reflect on the bang of their wins or losses. Winners smoke as much as losers at a betting shop, this is the observation. They would come out, light up, act serene or ogle their bet ticket. Make nervy conversation in two-word snatches:

'Fuckin scratched.'

'Jokin?'

'Minute before.'

'Mongrel.'

'Fuckin mongrel.'

When the next race started they would ditch their smokes and vanish back inside to make fists beneath the screens and stand agog. Events from multiple courses were shown, from Eagle Farm Racecourse to Happy Valley in Hong Kong, and races quickly followed one another. Sometimes this crew abandoned whole cigarettes. Few finished one to the end. Those screens in the shop showing races and prices were a window to God. Reality broke there before your eyes and carried your fate along with it, for immediate better or worse. All of us were humbled. We may never know if lightning will strike but we can know right away at a betting-shop screen which way our luck is running.

The minimum bet on a horse, dog or harness race was fifty cents. Fifty cents wasn't an incongruous sum for someone scavenging smokes. Fifty cents wasn't enough to buy anything in life, wasn't even a deposit on smokes. I could do fifty cents. And since it was all I had in life I felt I *should* do fifty cents. If I won I could buy the smokes, was the thinking. If I lost I was down fifty cents, no drama. Now I want to say here that I had never before and have never since scavenged for smokes, and even then wouldn't have dreamt of it outside the casino for instance, being a person of lofty standards. But it gives a sense of that homely outskirt atmosphere that it felt like par for the course there. Scavenging round the casino would make you a scavenger. Scavenging at the betting shop with fifty cents in your pocket made you a gambler with a sense of recycling.

Before long I was placing single bets of up to a hundred and twenty notes. This is usually where things get tense in a gambling story. This is where the trope goes down the slippery slope. But it's pertinent here because I had stumbled on a system for horses that gathered adjacent cascades into single bets, a system designed to hedge risks while playing for massive accumulated pots. It still either won or it didn't, but if you won, you won big, is the thing. And for my money, if you played it right, the odds were better than many a single bet. Those days I wore a pink and blue Hawaiian shirt which the surfing chef's mother had given him. He had been too horrified to wear it so he gave it to me as if it was his favourite shirt. I was so touched that he could be so untouched, that I wore it. And it was new after all. By about a decade later it had faded in just the right way and had come into fashion. I still have it. I backed that loser before it won, and that was just how this system was meant to work: it aimed to harness the losers. There I was with my shirt and my system betting against everyone else in the place, betting against human reason and memory, in a way, which is always a good bet. And while working on these cascades I also discovered how social gambling is in a betting shop. Gambling in our time of binary ethics, where everything's a crime on the news but loved by many, turned out to be social. A gathering of gamblers. A waggle of them. Adrenaline fosters rapport since you fret together, win or lose. You're gathered in trepidation, joy and angst, with numbness thrown in as a chaser. Sharing your pulse with strangers is highly social.

Next door in a similar brick low-rise with a small veranda was a real-estate office which our brains just filtered out. For all we knew it had exotic dancing. I can't even tell you what was on the other side. For betting patrons the whole world was just a wormhole to this urgent braying of races.

My little system grew itself organically, by instinct, while observing the maths in the betting shop. It seemed the first thing you needed in there was a gambling strategy, some decisions on how to spend your resources, which turned out to be easier the less resources you had. Because if you had a hundred bills it allowed more choices, but too many choices can fry your brain, they're the extra baggage of chance. In a fifty-cent shop you could fritter away your hundred on two hundred bets, the reality of which would be hour after hour of mood swings. That's called recreation. Or you could gamble half of it, and if you lost, use the other half to try and recover by way of more timid bets, which is the standard model for players without strategies. Its reality would be at least two sets of agony or anguish, and is called You Should Have Stayed at Home. Otherwise you could make yourself inwardly gasp at the unthinkable, which is really perfectly thinkable – plunge in and put it all as wisely as possible on a single big chance to change your life for the day. Agony or exhilaration. Ten minutes flat.

'Fortune favours the brave,' is what the regulars said as a mantra, and it's probably true. But here I felt attention needed to be paid to the wise part of the bargain. Someone was making a fortune at this and it didn't look much like us punters. I started watching this game like an umpire.

It doesn't take long to work out what's important in a horse's published form, and dogs you quickly learn are a crapshoot. Golden information on the nature of racing cascades is to be found in the punters' banter and in the off-handed racing commentary meant to kill time while a frisky horse holds up the field on its way to the gate. I learned for instance that greys aren't happy in strong sunshine, and that heavy ground makes the odds unstable. I learned that maiden races for two- and three-year-olds were used to assess them for handicapping, and this was key – if you believed the game was corrupt it meant good horses might be held back to avoid being heavily handicapped, which would also make the odds unstable. If you believed the game was fair it was still more unpredictable as the horses were newcomers, which by itself upset the odds. And that instability meant more long shots would win than the odds predicted. This is what I wanted.

Watching life in the betting shop I couldn't at first grasp

why so many of the crew bet on favourites and second-favourites for virtually no winnings, even when those horses still didn't come in half the time. Betting fifty bills to win seventy-five by backing a second-favourite, and then losing the fifty, seemed masochistic. But it supported my idea, because if you think about it, the winners of those bets are the bookmakers. The real money must essentially bet against favourites and hedge across the whole field. Watch those races: winner sixty-six to one, winner twenty-five to one, winner twelve to one. And in some of those races disruptions weren't just to win and place positions but were inversions of the whole field. Bookies must make their money doing what I proposed to do: pull cascades of chaos together and bet that the outcome will also be chaotic. It was a courting of natural uncertainty.

This was totalisator – tote – betting, so the odds changed right up to the start, according to the flow of wagers, compared to trackside bookies who could give you fixed odds. But it didn't matter to me, and even suited my system because while all the world tried to average their bets, I was going to back the improbable. In racing terms I wanted the Dave Graney cascade. I watched race after race through this negative prism and many results just didn't reflect odds given to those horses at the start.

Not to mention, I never figured out how a horse in a field of eight could attract odds of more than eight to one, sometimes up to dozens to one.

My regulars at the shop were open about their methods. There was a spectrum of styles in operation there. A span between picking horses by their names, and the final swamp of racing punters which is getting bogged down in the metrics of the form and then being surprised their choice didn't come in. But in that range some were playing more complex instruments. Aggregated chances like doubles and tricasts. You needed to pick multiple outcomes but they paid big.

On the other side of the non-existent-to-us real-estate building was a minor road heading back into the suburb of the railway cutting, at a right angle to the avenue; and on the other side of that road was a neighbourhood delicatessen. Marguerite with a modish gap in her front teeth was always there with a smile that said a surprise was in store, though there never was a surprise, I guess the smile was it.

This shop was the official vittler for the betting shop and, as such, a semi-sacred place. The shops fed each other well, they were companions of small change. Across that season I came to be known in the deli as part of the betting-shop crew, wearing my lurid shirt of the long-term investor. The hum of drinks chilling could make your pulse run steady. Air conditioning dampened unreason. The smell of sweets and the ghosts of baking pastry spoke of cosy brighter lives. Every so often I went to the shop to escape the hectic screens.

My thoughts were of conditions that could disrupt the odds in horse races, such as wind and rain. I was also beginning to notice how small maiden fields could be, with a dozen or less runners, often seven or eight. And I thought of the exotic instruments, not the double but the tricast, or trifecta. The trifecta is an accumulated pot of money given away to whoever picks the win, place and show of a race, that is, first, second and third places, in that order. It's long, long odds, but a single small bet will snag you the whole pot, unless by fluke you share the result with someone else. The pot routinely grew into the thousands.

To illustrate, a good race card that season looked like this:

Leyline Maiden Stakes 1000m

1.	Battimamselle	9/4
2.	Loopy Dog So	3–1
3.	Rediffusion	5–1
4.	Maco Line	7–1
5.	Goat Mout	12–1
6.	Pierrot Grenade	25–1
7.	Bamsee Fly	33–1
8.	Young Fridge	66–1

A tricast bet would have a unit on one horse to win, one to place and one to show, in the order picked. But they're hard to pick, the maths is more punishing than it looks. A better instrument to deal with it is the box tricast, or boxed trifecta. In this bet you pick any number of horses in a field at one unit each to win, place or show against all the other combinations. It's blackboard-level maths but the thing is to pick, say, six horses out of an eight-horse race, and if some come first, second or third in any order, you win the pot. Not being a fan of maths at the time I didn't look at the blackboard explanation, but it looks like this:

$$NH \times (NH - 1) \times (NH - 2) \times CC$$
(Where NH is number of horses and
CC is cost per combination)

So a six-horse combination to place in any order would look like this:

6 (horses) × 5 (horses) × 4 (horses) × 1 bet = Total cost of bet
(If the betting unit is £1 then this
would add up to a £120 bet)

Imagine this combination in a race with only eight runners. Chances are good that you can win the bet – the only moderator then is the starting price of the horses that win. If all the favourites come in as predicted, the payout is small and you lose out. But if the mules come in you win big and take home the tricast pot. This type of bet takes motivation, nerve, smokes and a steely gaze.

I won some money this way for a time. I gift you the info here. The season ended in better condition than it had started, since I paid some bills along the way. But like all things we propose to do in series, those bets were governed by two sets of odds: the first was attached to individual races, the second said, 'Do it again.' I paid bills with winnings along the way and kept too lean a bank. Betting strategy requires a bank to ride out dry spots caused by who's-your-daddy odds. That second set of odds is the problem set in gambling. I left the season gratefully, though, in my shirt. My crew is probably still there.

'Mongrel!'

Mission to Chutney

Perhaps Little Snake employs a spur that makes us want to engage with chance like that. An impetus whose pattern appears repeated across life, a two-part mechanism consisting of half future-oriented hope, and half uncomfortable, existing conditions which make it worth the plunge. A pull-push effect.

This one Saturday the surfers and I were propelled by an incitement to go out. The spur was made of hunger with a bright little spike in the form of an invitation. We needed a spur as it was ridiculous to get up and leave the house by ten on a groggy weekend morning after a big night out in the tropics. That was Berlin behaviour. But no, we got up and left the house and the sun was too bright and it was wrong. Although we stood on no ceremony the surfers were technically guests and we'd been invited to a radio station outside-broadcast party in a village in central Trinidad. We went because it was a chutney radio station. Chutney not the food but a steaming Trinidadian musical form blending local

East Indian vibes. Afro-Caribbean and Indian flavours have inter-bled here, and all these folks can dance. Chutney music mutated and twined its cascades till events like this can be a jangling ascension to a place where chaos makes sense.

But with the sun jackhammering down at ten o'clock Saturday morning it felt like getting up to visit a nail-clipper museum. It felt downright unwise and all the duty-free Gitanes Blondes Légères scattered around the bare house – multiple cartons as the place was big enough to need a convenient stash in every corner – suggested that we lie around and smoke them instead. Fashionably strewn, lightly worn clothes across the floor suggested staying in as well. Those jeans and shirts were harbingers of risk. I don't know why. Perhaps risk that if we got dressed and went outside we'd have a bad time. We'd have a bad time and have to be polite and it would still be before fucking midday.

Still, out we went and the existential spur, the call of the island regardless of our wishes, was that we had to leave the house. There was no food and there were no chairs and we could only live without the chairs. Long cascade. That being so, and being already out, we may as well go to a chutney fête before midday.

By eleven-thirty with half the crowd in tow we were clutching each other's forearms, barking at each other's faces and spinning in an ectoplasm of pulse and drums and hips and rum, swearing our allegiance to Laxmichand 'Babla' Virji Shah, Kumari Kanchan Dinkarrao Mali-Shah, to Heeralal Rampartap, Drupatee Ramgoonai, to plaid shirts, crooked teeth and longevity. Was it even possible to get this lit? More rum, hotter tracks and spiral-like kites with this crew. We may have never been this lit before midday in our lives.

The sun stood back and caressed without burning. We hadn't found chairs and we hadn't sourced food and those two failures were now the highest flame in the cascade. Drinking on empty, unable to sit and so dancing. We had left the house against our better judgement at the time and the risk had paid off in ascension. What the spur did was assume as a permanent state the weight of half the risk: we had to leave the house anyway. Once out then the destination could as well be anywhere, the major work of generating exit velocity was behind us. We were free. Chutney bacchanal.

The moral in practical terms: take the weight off some risk. Decide on a course of action of even worse consequence, then don't go there. Your position is suddenly lighter. Now it's back as a clear open space whose shine can lure new chances.

Pre-pay risk. Discover the confidence of less risk.

Is how it seemed after some chutney anyway.

Opalescence

But back to the serious business of work on the island. There was a time early on that I feel bad about. I came in with this parrot-or-die approach, with excess velocity, and trod too heavily around a quieter colleague who I didn't at first understand. Thankfully there was time – the situation needed it as one of us was peaceful and one of us was not, and we were at instinctive odds. But with time a glowing thing happened: I caught a heart-shine and understood this person all at once, at which admiration and affection grew. A quiet sentence spoken in conversation was a lucid key and we clicked into place right away. I can't repeat the comment or paint the person as they're a lover of peace and privacy. But a heart-shine. Remarkable and one of those biblical shifts that make us a collection of parables. The connection chilled me out. It wasn't mysterious, this was a spirit in clear existence that I had failed to spot. But then I did and our season changed and we can never turn back, and that interests us here.

As we speak of chaos and chance Little Snake tells us that all these people including me are swirling through these pages as agents of our own destiny, and we should look at some features of ourselves, not only as the agents of our outcomes but because people are also assessed and weighted with odds by others. Risk attaches to being a person among people much more than being a person alone.

We have all been at a beer shack in town where we get the lowdown from friends on a couple of local drinkers. Just as it happens all over, opinions and warnings and tips from trusted sources. Truth and bad-talk like tennis.

'Watch out for this one over here because of that dirt we heard about them; the other one's good though, we've met and they're stand-up.'

This other suit over here with the tie isn't someone we will like too much because he has a way of preening himself even though he's chilling with a drink at a bar, and not even a bar but a beer shop. Someone however will like him very much, and we could probably like him on a different day in a different beer shop.

And so a model emerges from these persons at the beer shop, possibly a big enough model to explain all persons and society and books and art. In the model we're all here at the beer shop, which is physical and metaphysical, which is seedy but beloved and thumping with bass, and we're standing around. Although they've never met before and Person Number One doesn't warm to Person Number Four. But Person Number Three gets a vibe from Person Number Five, and while Person Number Two has the dirt on Person Number Four, he finds that when he's standing there within eyeball range he's inclined to find the person sympathetic.

So each person has caught a shine off someone else in the shop, not necessarily the same person, and some don't catch a shine at all. One person will bad-talk another two while one of those two will talk about one of the bad-talkers in a good light, but will speak in a bad light about one of the people the bad talker speaks well of.

Tell me if it doesn't seem we can explain this by opalescence: depending on where you stand you will see a different set of colours. Your sister goes out with a dick and you can't understand it – but he opalesced to her, she caught some colours you didn't catch. And maybe she angled herself not only to receive the shine of others but to transmit her own shine to the world. And only those with colour showing would come together after events had angled them to put their shines in touch. Others were left indifferent or even repulsed by the lack of an answering heart-shine. And so the world at this beer shop was governed by the probability of one person's colours transmitting to another.

We opalesce. Collins describes it as a 'milky iridescence', Merriam-Webster says 'to exhibit a play of colours like those of an opal'. But this is what we seem to do in the beer shop, this is for all intents and purposes how we are, and those flashes can pass us by or pull us in or be completely absent. Opal rock without colour is called potch and a majority of opal rock is without colour. The more colour it gets the more valuable it grows, exponentially so, and the more amazing it's perceived as for its fire.

And so it seems in the beer shop.

Seems after these beers anyway.

Kabuki Faces

In the shadows away from the drinkers in the soft Trinidadian night roamed creatures from other realities. *Churiles*, which were the spirits of women who had died in childbirth. They would wail and prey on other expectant women as well as on the men who had treated them badly. There roamed *La Diablesse*, whose face was of a corpse hidden under a wide-brimmed hat with a veil. *La Diablesse* had one cloven foot which she hid under her skirts as she targeted men at local dances, luring one of them out into the night to accompany her home. By the time they saw the cloven foot and realised their mistake she had abandoned them in the forest where they would die.

There were *Douens*, which were the spirits of children who had died before baptism; there was *Mama Dlo*, who had the upper body of a beautiful woman and the torso of an anaconda. Hunters could hear her tail smacking the surface of languid pools. Needless to say, by our thinking today it's pretty much impossible to be seduced out of a dance to a slow confusing death by someone whose cloven hoof you didn't spot in time. But the point is it isn't. Remember Ramona in Tobago. These mythologies are complex placeholders which offer sensory experience instead of the usual statistics for horrors in life, and these stories portend realistic human outcomes such as being haunted by the death of a child. They are polished cascades describing long-odds menaces. *Mythomatics*. And the truth is there are many more terrifying things in reality than facing a human anaconda, and many more rococo ways to die than being led astray by *La Diablesse*.

But according to Little Snake we've thrown our vivid and emotionally practical mythology away with our childhood and adopted statistics instead: in modern thought the odds of someone deliberately leading you astray in a forest after a dance are longer than a million to one. The odds of being born with anything resembling a hoof are longer than a million to one. The odds of being born with a hoof, becoming a corpse and then luring someone into the forest are longer than billions to one. So we discard the notion as fantasy.

But remember Ramona/*La Diablesse*. Luring men away from a dance. To knowingly lead them astray to their possible deaths. Men who failed to see the death in her eyes. She must have kept it metaphorically under her veil along with her corpse face. Behold this accurate myth.

We should wonder if we already know all this, deep down. Wonder if we got scared about it and stopped referring to it, if we have lost the strength to contemplate the horrors of nature's maths. The maths of pathos and beauty and menace. We tossed our mythology out with storybooks and toys, and consigned our shivers to the fantasy of childhood. But we still shiver. And looking at the stats of dances and forests and hooves is no use whatsoever. Nothing in science will give us a taste of horror's next algorithm. Vivid folklore will.

I seem to remember that most of the island's alter-beings had their antidotes. If you came upon *Mama Dlo* in the woods you were to remove your left shoe, turn it upside down and walk backwards all the way home. There was no superhero to wrap you in his cloak while he vanquished all comers, apart from one *Dee Baba* who accepted offerings such as tobacco, rum, whisky or dope to protect your land from danger. Heeding the vision, applying the antidote and being your own quiet hero is brave enough.

Imagine the people who missed or resisted Ramona. Who sensed things weren't right. Who heard about her later and felt the shiver. But for their lucky, heroic or wise navigation of Ramona they would have been consigned paradoxically to being both a statistic and a myth. There are no superheroes in reality but there are brave people.

Mythical codes that help us interpret reality must still lurk in the hearts of people, and metrics on paper do nothing to replace or allay them. Our mythologies have been down-sold to a fantasy media who tries to disturb us with off-the-rack plots. The shiver was divested of its purpose. Look how we still pine for it, still remember it. The obsessional pastime of not walking on paving cracks is a tiny gamble for huge wins and losses in our mythological memory palace. A game of minor skill but an unnecessary risk, if only in the mind, is the point. Do we test the risk in order to call the shiver back? Metrics tell us we could continue walking on cracks and still have a better life, which in turn would throw up its own real risks. But we set ourselves a pointless challenge: if I touch a crack *La Diablesse* will track me down. Then we touch the damn crack and say: Okay best of three.

This is us and we don't want things too simple or sterile, our myth-world carries on trading in shivers no matter the language or numbers we use. If we think about it the great lamas of Tibet are special because they can do it simply. There's the gold standard. That's how difficult it is. They send scouts to the farthest countryside to hunt down souls reincarnated into infants who can understand not to care about cracks in the pavement. Meanwhile we satisfy our innate unsimpleness with risk. We call up the shiver in an organised way and that way is called gambling.

If the only fear we're born with is the fear of darkness, since it's always unknown it must grow to include the jungle of odds. Anything could and does lurk and loom. Moreover the odds we most worry about are the odds of our death. The final boss of odds, whether Little Snake comes around or not. And in the shadow of this hammer-blow of odds we still test and test and test our chances. Our gambles may be a whole-food containing the protein of death; and while we wait for that inevitability we convert the aminos to propel our cascades. Whether or not we're born aware of primal darkness, it's the source of a built-in lifelong shiver, our only one. This makes every life heroic.

My first hero when I was little was Shintaro. He was a samurai who was always battling the Iga Ninja on TV. Always busy trying to stay a step ahead. He spent much of his time in robes among people pulling kabuki faces of implausible melodrama. Sharp inward gasps and open-mouthed terror made Shintaro my homie because I also pulled kabuki faces and I knew the melodrama to be plausible. Being born was surprising enough never mind the rest of this Buñuel epic. As a child I knew kabuki to be an accurate expression of the facts of life, and the only adults in the world who agreed with me were Shintaro and his crew.

Observe babies: see how they're made of pure feeling. They're said to be unfiltered and one thing this means is extravagant facial expressions. A baby's face can shift in an instant from joy to trepidation to horror. And I say they don't pull this face for exercise or fun, they pull it due to a gust of existential terror passing through them, perhaps a colic in their tender systems that puts them in fear for their lives. This is babies being pure and unfiltered and the condition persists through early childhood. Then at a certain point it becomes wise to stop this revelation of feeling. It's important in our grown-up animal self to be cool and this means we curate ourselves in front of others. The faces dissolve but the feelings go on inside.

Because what if kabuki feelings never stop? And mythomatical sensors in the system are suppressed so as not to alarm ourselves or passers-by. With the pretence that we can have mastery over chaos.

Kabuki isn't fiction, it's non-fiction. About our real inner state, about the infant we left howling at the gate of things, about what happened to the fucking womb let alone this ambush; and it comes with catastrophic rattles and thumps and chimes and drums and unearthly hoots and squeals and yet is beautiful in an icy way like a fish flashing underwater. This is what seems to go on. In the place where shivers are born. Where the cloven hoof, the corpse's face, the human anaconda and the unbaptised child are understood. And all psychological study is an attempt to understand how kabuki got the faces just right.

Shintaro stopped appearing around the time my kabuki faces withdrew, and that was about the time I sat at the top of the stairs in my parents' house and prepared to throw a chair at a snake.

Shintaroo! they used to call him on the TV, beseeching: *Shintarooo!*

If when we learn that others want to master us we hide our kabuki self because it shows our fear and hurt, then our gambles in life – perhaps especially the unwise and compulsive ones – might be its grasping hand, its cry.

Je suis Shintaro. Cry out loud next time you play: *Shintaro!*

Signals From the Jungle

No matter how dull and mathsless the places we come from appear, we already know vivid maths – because we listen to music and music is pure vivid maths. We understand the code without thinking. We feel it. Sometimes we even know which song will play before it plays. We feel the maths change in the air. This is how connected we are to music. I wonder if it exists in the abstract, or if it comes into being as we're becoming emotionally receptive, translating maths into feeling reality. A signal from the jungle, a vivid maths pulse.

One thing's for sure: we follow like bamsee flies.

It also comes with its kismet. Heading west towards Macqueripe along the coast from Port of Spain, now that Dave Graney has made it out of the deck, the Brahms violin concerto plays in the car. The island is a breeding ground for musical styles but classical isn't one you hear much. I suspect the tropics aren't an easy place for some instruments to live. So the Brahms violin concerto is conspicuous, a teasing coincidence which doesn't necessarily blend with rum shacks and coconut vendors. Still it's a kabuki cry from the soul, as primal and affecting as a muezzin's call to prayer, and I'm trying it out on a work colleague who doesn't appear to be listening as we float along past the yacht club. The violin soars high into a solo, and he says: 'Boy plays a mean harmonica.'

Months later up by the corner of Carlos and Roberts streets in rustic Woodbrook with its gingerbread houses and low-rise palms I heard the Brahms concerto again and stopped in my tracks. It was coming from thin air and I looked around and eventually there, almost out of sight in the shade of the Brooklyn Bar, a man, the only patron because it was early in the day, was playing a fiddle.

This was Brahms and his influence on those island days.

The cowabunga came soon after as if to confirm that we're right to wonder.

My mother blew through with an aunt on their way to a less vibrant island, that is to say less edgy. And thinking about it, it was in my household in Mexico as a kid that my ear for varied music, including classics, was tuned. My mother's favourite piece had been Richard Addinsell's 'Warsaw Concerto' – high succulent romance, a soundtrack not a concert piece – and I only ever heard it at home, its age was long past by then to hear it anywhere else. But I heard it once more, just once, the only other time I can remember outside of home. When these ladies turned up on their flying visit – their first ever in the region – I took them to an open-air bar opposite Queen's Park Cricket Club in Port of Spain. And by the time the first drinks were fixed, from the still night air came the strains of the 'Warsaw Concerto'. We couldn't believe it. It was played on steel drums, not a pair or a handful but over fifty of them, a symphony orchestra of steel pans rehearsing in a pan-yard next door. We took our drinks and relocated like zombies to sit in the pan-yard; and as we stepped through the gate we had to pause for a man striding past in a shirt featuring one bold word: 'MEXICO'.

And this is the thing: Little Snake doesn't suggest it was a paranormal event. No, no, Little Snake tells us, this is a mathematical occurrence. A *coincidence*. And so be it, the more experiences we have in life the more their echoes will play. But some of what we're looking at suggests a clustering of coincidence into the kismet-rich environments or times we're calling vivid maths. Little Snake says this to maths: there can also come a moment in unfolding reality when a statistical explanation is no more plausible than a paranormal explanation. This is what we're here to explore. And our only bitch at science is for its refusal to admit to reality the things its tools can't yet define. Hence we're here proposing new tools, or at least reconditioning old ones.

That night was the last time I ever heard the concerto with my mother. And the only time I ever heard it in public. The soundtrack to the long cascade.

The Soucouyant

Travelling from east to west through Port of Spain there were seven good bars or clubs to frequent. Each had its flavour and time; Trinidad is too rare to deal with sober. Today I use those same seven clubs as a memory device; I got tired of scribbling notes in bed after ideas followed me up the stairs that had been absent when I was at work. So I use the memory of those places to store notes, one each, east to west, and in the morning I go back and see if I left anything there in mind. But the existential rub of these clubs was that sometimes you'd go to bed happy, as it were, or you might occasionally wake up with the mystery bruise or scrape that is the hallmark of a long good night. Drinking is different in the tropics, I suspect humid air hydrates us as we drink – capacity increases.

So I woke up one morning after a night out to find my pillow half soaked in blood. Not super-fresh and not old, middle-of-the-night type blood. Half the pillowcase, no joke. Apart from a little groggy I felt fine and this was perplexing.

Forced to get up and check myself for injuries I examined my nose first, as it seemed to me the only likely source of this much blood not caused by a gunshot. Blood will run easy in tropical heat, although I'm not prone to nosebleeds. But my face seemed clear and the rest of me too. Cleaning up left no evidence of a wound that I could see. I was fine was the main thing, so I left it at that. Any injury would make itself just as well known after coffee. I brought the pillow down and ditched it. It was also mysterious for being a benign way to meet a lot of your own blood. And it wasn't the worst thing I'd woken up to after a drink. There was a marvellous storming lady with eyes as bright as steel who came up to do some housework, and who let herself in with an old radio stuck on full volume, shrieking: *Jesus is the winner man, the winner man, the winner man, Jesus is the winner man* down in the bowels of this cavernous echoing place and no offence to Jesus but I knew I was damned.

When I told colleagues that our Friday drink had left me bleeding they didn't think for a second, they hissed right away: *A soucouyant!*

A soucouyant was a spirit – a *jumbie* – in the form of a haggard old woman by day who could shed her skin and turn into a fireball at night, flying around to suck the blood of sleeping victims. To extinguish a soucouyant you had to find the mortar into which she'd folded her empty skin and treat it with coarse salt; the skin would shrink, she wouldn't fit back and she would perish. The advice was to empty sacks of rice around your house or at a crossroads leading to your place, as she was compelled to gather rice grain by grain, giving you the chance to search for her empty skin. Now, being scientific I naturally sought second and third opinions – but whenever I mentioned the pillow of blood I heard *soucouyant* without hesitation, and with no particular horror or awe. The consensus on the street as far as remedies went was simpler than sacks of rice or finding her empty skin: just having salt by the bed would apparently do it, so I went to the market and bought some salt with only half my tongue in my cheek, because hey – local maths. And that single-participant clinical trial showed a hundred-per-cent effectiveness in that I never woke up to find blood on my pillow again.

And what are the odds for that? says Little Snake.

I had notched up my first island soucouyant event, which made me virtually local; but I was reminded that there were more demons still to watch out for, and perhaps more shivers to come. There was still *La Diablesse* who we hadn't seen at the chutney dance, although what undead soul was going to get out of bed at ten in the morning to drag their cloven hoof out dancing?

And would we have even known if *La Diablesse* or Ramona were in the room? It goes to a broader question, which if you chase it far enough is a complication to all ideas of probability for all sentient beings: what about the risks we're unaware of? All our questions and calculations relate to identified risks; but what if other lotteries are playing behind them with infinite options to replace or skew the risks we identified? Current laws of physics as they relate to unfolding reality suggest that all possible risks, and even all possible outcomes, may be lined up all ready to go in the world of probability. Our interaction with our cascade forces probability to choose one outcome.

But in this case the outcome was a soucouyant – using the name as a placeholder for whatever truly caused this blood – a phenomenon I'd never heard of before, and a risk which would never have entered my mind. When I awoke to see all this blood I immediately weighed the odds against a list of known risks: nosebleed, mouthbleed, haemorrhage, unseen open wound. But my list was quickly exhausted without identifying any cause. And here's the Little Snake angle, perhaps this is what we take away: across my varied life lived in a number of places and cultures the list of risks I had compiled for unexplained blood did not cover this event.

But every local I spoke to knew exactly what had happened. Is this Little Snake's example of local maths?

Mighty Viper

The Gulf of Paria where Port of Spain sits is like a shallow inland sea infused with mud from the Orinoco delta across the way, plus the Amazon further down. Dotted with rusty freighters and Chinese crews and stirred by manatees and tarpons. To find a sandy beach you have to drive a little, and if you go over the mountains behind Port of Spain you come to picture-postcard Maracas Bay. Largely undeveloped except to facilitate food and cold beer. The flaxen crescent of sand lies under palms like eyelashes against deep-set forested slopes.

Going to the beach was a cyclic occurrence like a pulse across those years, being the first place I had been taken to on the weekend of my arrival on the island. And where by fluke while neck-deep in water, I met important new colleagues and friends. It was also one of the last places I went before leaving the island, plus I beat a rhythm in between by taking occasional visitors to quench their island tropes. There was a surfable little shorebreak in the middle of the bay, but Maracas was mostly for swimming, meaning when I took the surfers they spent the day conspiring to lift the swell by dropping a bus two hundred yards out.

The first view of Maracas, one of the lushest views of a bay you'll see, comes from a lookout on the approaching road high up the mountain behind. The lookout is a compelling enough stop that traders set up with trinkets and food, and sometimes you'll find a calypsonian – a *chantwell* – with a guitar. On one occasion the calypsonian was Mighty Viper, a founding local voice of calypso, someone I'd already seen at a hangout in town. The old troubadour always carried a photo album taped up with plastic like an heirloom that featured pictures of him in his halcyon days singing for Princess Margaret of England. This was his CV and he made sure you took it in before he pitched you a song. But here's where this Mighty-Viper-beach-detour is headed: once you exhausted your memory of calypso requests, as predictably in my case with 'Matilda' – 'she take me money and run Venezuela' – he would ask your name and provenance to extemporise a song on the spot.

Now, extempo is a celebrated branch of calypso, but if we put aside any blank verses these artists might use as templates, there's also a tiny model for us that reveals how probability chooses some outcomes over others. A mini maquette of the jungle. Every year at carnival time an extemporised calypso death-match leads to an Extempo Monarch being crowned, and those artists serve up some lyrical outcomes you wouldn't expect. You wonder if even they can predict what will come out of their mouths, and even if they can I want to flag this idea: Mighty Viper's extempo gigs on the lookout seem like a working human model of the forces of probability we're looking at. While probability may be poised with options ready to land, what we observe is that it doesn't seem to pick one until the moment it's demanded. As if nothing is formed until it needs to be. Likewise, Mighty Viper has the words in his mind like unassigned particles but they only fall together once the song is starting to be sung. And here's the problem for Einstein's universe where reality is supposedly pre-authorised by science like credit card debt: if your name happened to be Gizmo Bizmo and you came from Kamchatka, then Mighty Viper's lyrics – some of which he'd never thought of before, having never bumped into your name – would have to somehow already exist. When the truth would be that Viper was hearing at least some of those lyrics for the first time ever himself. And if he never ran across Gizmo, or if Gizmo didn't purchase a song, the lines would never be formed. We should call some calypso rhythms to mind and look into this science around the Viper – another snake of a different hue on the mathscapade.

The Mighty Viper will also demonstrate this science better than Erwin Schrödinger did, although for reference we'll start with Schrödinger and his mad thought-experiment. While chewing the fat with Einstein in 1935, Schrödinger was tucking into Nils Bohr's and Werner Heisenberg's Copenhagen interpretation of quantum mechanics, which says that a particle can be two things at once until someone observes it, at which point it fixes a final outcome. *Our observation causes it to choose*, and Schrödinger pitched this paradox to show how absurd the theory sounded.

Recall the experiment: a live cat is sealed in a box with a radioactive source, a vial of poison and a radioactivity detector such as a Geiger counter. We can't see any of it from outside the box. If or when the detector picks up any radioactivity in the box it will shatter the vial and release the poison which will kill the cat. But according to the Copenhagen interpretation the cat is both fully alive and dead until our observation forces reality to collapse into one outcome or the other. It follows then that, left unobserved, the cat exists in two states at once.

Now: if we were near the box the cat could mew and give itself away, hence it's only a thought-experiment. But Schrödinger hadn't met the Mighty Viper: because in our island thought-experiment Gizmo's extempo calypso song also both exists and doesn't exist, until either Gizmo turns up and we hear the song, or the Mighty Viper dies without singing it. It's not quite the cat experiment but a child of the same idea, and is closer to the path we're on: what are the odds of Gizmo turning up? What then are the odds of Gizmo buying a song? What are the odds of us finding Gizmo and paying for the song, or of us telling Viper our name is Gizmo? All these options and more for the birth of a Gizmo song exist as probabilities around the Mighty Viper as we face him at the lookout. And we can't know the outcome until we know.

In gambling terms the cascade would not be visible to bet on until we knew that Gizmo was en route to the lookout and Viper was there. And like all gambles it would be an all-or-nothing bet: the song would be sung or not.

Back with our scientists, it was also Erwin Schrödinger who chose the word *entanglement* to describe apparently separate particles behaving as one; and it was Einstein who coined the term *spooky action at a distance* to describe entangled particles when they were separated across space, even across the farthest reaches of the universe, while essentially being the same particle. So if you observed one and it chose a reality, say a clockwise or a counter-clockwise spin, its partner across space would do the same, instantly and without communication. All because the particle had been observed.

One upshot of the Copenhagen interpretation must be that if we don't observe things they remain probabilities and don't choose outcomes. But in the Relative State Formulation proposed twenty-five years later by Hugh Everett III, those particles don't pick a single reality – they collapse into every possibility at once. And that theory proposes an answer to one far-out factor: if a particle in two places at once can instantly change to the same thing when observed, even across the universe, it means there can be no distance between them. Distance is time and it would take billions of light years for one to learn what the other was doing. Which can only mean they're in the same place. The Relative State Formulation says they're in parallel worlds, and when different possibilities exist in breaking reality, each turns into a new reality and branches into a universe of its own. This also means we can't die, essentially because at least one probability would always lead to our survival.

Other recent theories have it that multiple worlds were already in existence, that weirdo quantum behaviour is down to them talking among themselves. But however these theories differ, they all recognise one thing: that upon driving to Maracas Bay we may have stopped at the lookout and found the Mighty Viper, we may have not stopped and found the Mighty Viper, we may have driven the wrong way, we may have hit an agouti in the road, or we may have overshot a corner and destroyed the car. Theories only differ in whether one of those things happened or all of them happened at once.

It's twisted maths and we could write it off as bullshit if quantum mechanics wasn't so notable among sciences for so far having none of its theories contradicted by results from live experiments; including more recent experiments which finally showed that quantum entanglement at a distance exists.

But there's something else in these quantum ideas that fits with our clunky old road trip here. As we look at humans and creatures, at our energies and cascades, tell me if these quantum templates don't seem to fit our personal dynamics much better than metrical ones, where we always seem to be wrong or at odds with everything. For instance, quantum mechanics uses the term *decoherence* to describe the disconnect between weird unfolding quantum life and what appears to finally happen in the everyday world, where our pasta still hasn't arrived and we're full of breadsticks. Now I have on occasion collapsed into a state outside myself, we've all been decoherent, let's admit it, even incoherent, and full of wild unformed probabilities, even driven crazy by designs that haven't been forced to a choice. So maybe we're internally decoherent all the time, maybe we live on the quantum side of coherence, where the free-form world of subconscious mythology collapses trying to fit the holes of this stricter classical reality. It could explain how twisted things can get between our choices and their outcomes in the 'real world'.

Swirling micro-whims could potentially be anything at all until we pick one and act. And this applies very clearly to the gambles we've been talking about. Before we toss the dice we are both winners and losers. Even the lottery scratchcard could for all intents and purposes before it's scratched be anything, although it's an objective pre-printed number that's simply obscured – but from Nils Bohr's point of view it is both a winner and a loser until we observe it. According to Everett we will simultaneously win and lose every prize as well as be stalked by the cashier, who possibly has a cloven hoof. And according to some newer theories we'll drive by later, the outcomes might depend on our subjective belief in the probability of what might happen, which offers new food for thought on beginner's luck and positive outcomes flowing from confidence. What if, on top of mathematical functions in the science of breaking reality, these theories could also explain humanity's persistent preference for ideas and mythologies over statistics?

I could recall prior accidental experience of quantum change from times and places before cascades came to mind. Sure, it's easy to overlay patterns on everything after the fact but there *were* existing patterns there, and after all, according to pretty much every system of thought, we're here to work stuff out and to apply what we find to the future. Our master-cascades tumble on as experiments, where even accidental prior incidents are deposited into unawareness accounts as events to rediscover and interpret later on. They must be important markers in our charting of cascades; even if we experience them looking ahead muttering *what the fuck?* – later, looking back, we often make sense of them. And it can only hone our situational radar to try to soar on a cascade's thermals like an eagle without falling off.

This is how beatific ideas can get on the beach, anyway. Might as well write them into a song for acoustic guitar. Might as well give them to Mighty Viper:

Look on de beach for de one dey call Pierre,
Musing all day and never move his derrière,
Well any fool knows dat smart action is key,
But he confused beer with philoso-pheee ...

You wouldn't say any of this in a bar, for instance, where good humour demands some derision of life. But on our vivid road trip we can speak without the shadow of fashionable cynicism upon us, the stain that stops us using words like 'joy'. At any rate, before these ideas were hatched, before Little Snake and Mighty Viper, I recall I once inadvertently placed a kind of quantum bet on a horse race live at the track. A model of one at least. I drove to Los Angeles from up the coast one early summer's night under a typical mauve sky, with a cool partner, though things were going badly between us, which I'll take the hit for. We found a mediocre hotel near the racetrack for the night, and went over to the track because things were going poorly and why not. At the track things briefly went better with dressed-up folks around, echoing announcements, and with a drink at the bar positive adrenaline came around. I found a bookie and laid a bet, a single cowabunga to end bad times. But things got worse between us before the race was run, and we had to bail out. Back under palms and a purple sky to the hotel with its sound of ice-makers.

And we left. I never saw the upshot of the race.

Afterwards I made a point of not looking it up.

According to everything above – it's a winner.

A quantum nest-egg.

The story at once has a moral, no morals and infinite morals. If Bohr and Heisenberg are right the bet was a winner at least until we left the hotel. I'll never know the outcome either way. It might still be a winner today, although any loss would have been observed at the time by objective witnesses; but I haven't since observed those observers. If Everett is right there's a parallel universe where I'm living it up in LA. And if Einstein is right I would have been better off giving the money to Viper and telling him my name was Gizmo.

One Thing About Bohr, Though

That the building blocks inside the building blocks of everything can be in two places at once is a modern fact. And that our ideas are unreliable when we have drinks on board is another modern fact.

But science is looking again. Research is starting to show that drink and drugs loosen our focus in the mind, making it slip between ideas and speed towards new connections. So as we pit our rum-fuelled road trip against the geniuses of science, before we start to feel like that one fucked-up uncle or aunt at the wedding, I want us to remember one thing: the Carlsberg brewery in Copenhagen gave Nils Bohr a house next door with a direct pipeline of beer. Gave it to him. And after living there with a direct pipeline of beer for five years Bohr's work on quantum really took off, not least with his theory of complementarity.

A *pipeline* of fucking beer.

Just saying.

Bird Pepper

So much information across this season came bundled in hot choppy air through an open car window as immoderate plant-life flashed by. Colleagues, proud of their island and excited to show it off, used our road trips here and there to tell its secrets of darkness and light, its vivid curiosities. One such from a colleague was the lore surrounding Trinidad's coveted bird pepper. I like hot pepper, I have tolerance and I enjoy it just like swearing, for giving time the teeth to bite back. And Trinidad is home to super-hot peppers as well as good fiery curses.

The bird pepper topic comes up along the road to central Trinidad, which they conveniently call Central, same way they call the south 'Sout'. Our destination is a stand-alone family restaurant on the edge of a grassy clearing where cricket is sometimes played and where a hen or even a cow might stray. We're back with the roosters and wood smoke, and the word is that we're about to taste the best curried shrimp in existence. Having by now tried the best duck, conch, goat and channa aloo, I don't suspect the promise is exaggerated, even though the colleague might have a thing for one of the establishment's daughters.

As I understand the bird pepper story, it's not about the birds-eye chili which is common in Asian kitchens – the first thing a search will throw up – but a rare local pepper which apparently only grows after the seed has been eaten, digested and shat back out by a bird. Whatever variety of pepper this is, it has achieved almost mythical status, as if getting yourself a bird pepper tree is a lottery win from the deepest jungle of maths.

A bird has to eat a bird pepper seed then drop it over your yard, and it may even have to be a particular species of bird, who knows, local information is scarce. Rumour has it that this magically flavoured, searing hot pepper favours bedding itself in the south of the island. There's a story about a human skeleton found in a forest up behind Port of Spain, a skeleton which everyone knew must have come from the south because a bird pepper grew from its backside. So this legendary pepper is a lottery prize and the source of much local debate. Information from one new source suggests it can also be grown from harvested seed, but that you must pick the donor pepper under a Pisces moon, plant it under a Pisces or Scorpio moon, transplant it by moonlight, et cetera. Little Snake suggests the odds are as good to simply wait for the bird. 'People live and die without seeing a bird pepper tree,' says my colleague.

So bird pepper is another vivid model on the maths-capade, which interests us here as getting a bird pepper tree doesn't call for a single stroke of luck: it needs a cascade of them. The odds begin with a bird even finding a fruit to eat from such a rare plant, and if those plants are such a blessing then we can imagine their owners don't leave the peppers lying around. The bird has to be in the vicinity of a bird pepper with some viable seed, and has to eat that pepper. Then and only then come the odds of where it will drop the seed. We can imagine this will be a smallish bird, and we know that the smaller the bird, the faster its digestion. According to James Stevenson's work on the digestion of food in small birds, it could have an average digestion time of an hour and thirty-two minutes. So unless a bird flies direct to your yard after eating the pepper, you can't live far from the source.

Then comes the applied maths of target size, where in this instance fortune favours the rich, as the bigger your plot of land the more likely the bird will hit it. The final maddening odds apply to that dropping, and it can't be any old shit, it has to be bird pepper shit. All these odds transpire in the maths-jungle's darkness; as we might be aware of shitting birds in general but we'll be unaware of bird-pepper-shitting birds, given that their world is as anonymous as the internet.

It's likely we'll only find out when the plant starts showing fruit.

At which we should go out and buy a lottery ticket, or not, depending on whether you feel the luck has come or was spent on the tree and gone.

I say it as lotteries could be modelled on bird-pepper-tree events. Picking six out of forty-nine numbers is a cascade that has to line up precisely, bang-bang-bang-bang-bang-bang in a cumulative series, where each extra step exponentiates the odds of hitting the next. The last mathematician I heard on the subject said we could expect to win a lottery jackpot once every thirty thousand years if we played every draw. The numbers from jungle and mangrove seem to converge when they get this long, as the bet grows to such long odds that the maths required to calculate winning the next draw are as scary as the maths for winning it at all.

When it gets to this many zeros we have to call it luck. We need to throw arithmetic out of the window and take a closer look at this. Because it doesn't even seem to be one thing, in a way. It looks more like a trinity, as if there's passive luck and active luck and then maths sitting up at the apex. Perhaps they can work individually or together. By passive luck I mean the count-your-blessings variety that runs on relativity and interpretation to make us feel lucky to have two eyes and arms and legs, and enough food on our plate. Active luck is the often-ironic fortune that metes out favours, calamity and surprise on any scale, and which reeks of quantum again as it deals with vigorous choices that can mostly only be marvelled at in retrospect – BANG! They're done. Then there's maths running the chances that build our cascades. That maths pays out from time to time in other ways whether we like it or not, so I'm not sure we can call it pure luck. Things only get interesting when both passive and active luck are involved, and I want to propose that they're particulate, since their outcomes seem to spin and bounce around.

With the bird pepper tree in mind I recall a story that we can use in place of a Hadron Collider to lure and observe a lottery's particles in action. The story is a prequel to the horse racing season we explored in an earlier cascade, when I needed cash badly and by yesterday. Youth is like that all by itself, but this was youth and trouble on steroids, a time of life when the end loomed near and you saw yourself in the grave still needing the same cash. Bite marks on the coffin lid.

But there was a deal to be made with the universe and I made that deal when I had to. As a pledge of devotion the deal demands that we abandon pride and shame and get inventive. That we pray for luck and envision it. That we dream it into our pores. And I did this, not for anything constructive but to backfill urgent debt. I didn't have seed money, not a fraction of what I needed, I was down to small change. And there came a day when I could either buy a can of tuna and a pack of noodles or a lottery ticket. Well, if you need half a million bucks and only have two dollars, the matter answers itself. At that level of the game, zero is a more powerful position than two. Having zero is to have everything to live for; having two is to be badly off.

I bought the lottery ticket. For the sake of romance I'd like to say I went hungry, but in truth I had enough change left over for noodles by themselves. Still those times were a slippery wedge of what felt like last possible chances in life, a cascade of all-or-nothing days. This particular day I walked to buy this ticket because I didn't have a car, and I walked farther than I needed to so I could buy it in the environment with which I felt the most rapport, the luckiest-feeling environment, which in that neighbourhood at that time was the newsagent. I don't think I thought about this at the time but this is what happened, autopilot thought about it and sent me to the newsagent.

Binding-glue and printing ink smell lucky, they always smelled lucky to me. Even so, the newsagent wasn't all beer and skittles compared to the delicatessen, for instance. The choice came with its pains as there were crisp new papers and magazines that I coveted but I could not afford to buy. When you don't have the small things that sparkle with civilisation they grow more glaring and valuable. Nothing says things are fine like a crisp newspaper or magazine, along with the peace to cradle them in your hands and drink them in. Pure passive luck. There were also fresh books on the shelves and I'm a sucker for books. Books are lucky and I want them whether I read them or not. If I could have bought a book it would have transported me into another life where I wasn't walking around in a daze trying to get lucky with extremely long odds. Stupid odds.

But in terms of those odds I made a decision, one I recommend to anyone pursuing the lifestyle of a rescue dog: the real key to luck when you're at this point of the wedge is to ignore the maths altogether. Not even just ignore but disbelieve it. This strategy must be behind the saying 'it's better to be lucky than intelligent'. It must mean 'put intelligence aside if you want to be lucky'. And I did that. I didn't know the maths behind the lottery at the time, and just as well. This is where quantum ideas can serve us, Bohr's name has sparked a quantum cascade through this chapter; in retrospect what I seemed to be doing instinctively while choosing to bury my head in the sand was to conceive of luck as an atomic particle, demonstrating all the behaviour of an entangled photon, and subject to the same paradoxical laws. If I observed my own situation it might change states into something more probable, which would mean losing – when what I needed was the highly improbable, which was a win. It makes me want to say: if you ever found yourself instinctively flinching away from a situation with multiple possible outcomes, instead of labelling it 'avoidance behaviour' why not ask if it is actually an innate sympathy with, and understanding of, the ways of quantum life. We're all built of the same stuff after all, as solid and sparse and electrical, literally stardust. And perhaps we should remember: while our current times are all about having more numbers in front of us and running human life with binary logic, civilisation is as harrowing and fucked up as it ever was.

Less observation also puts the onus on internal *creation* – creation of will, thought, hope, imagery and energy. And these have never seemed a bad idea to generate. So first step: I left the odds unexamined, and in a state of limbo visualised winning numbers. I picked my own numbers; anybody who's won a jackpot more than once will tell you quick picks are bad maths. Then I put the ticket in my pocket and later over curry noodles I wished on it.

If enchanted desperation amounts to a model by which we can examine quantum physics, I feel Little Snake would understand. Perhaps we sense here some really useful depths in science that aren't being discussed in schools due to education budgets having been slashed. But there is one interpretation of quantum mechanics known as QBism, a branch of quantum Bayesianism, which proposes that a quantum state such as those we've been talking about is not an element of reality – instead it's the degree of belief we have in the outcome of our measurement. So every probability is a measure of our belief in an outcome.

And this rides close to our inquiry into risk.

It's been called anti-realism and has its share of critics, some arguing that the theory adds nothing to the untangling of quantum paradoxes. But quantum paradoxes are pretty resistant to untangling; this is the place after all where things change when we observe them: the moment of manifestation. Others accuse the theory of solipsism, which is headed towards the idea that nothing may exist objectively anyway. But it just suits us here. I mean: if we could find the timbre, the tenor, the charge, the current, the maths, the spirit, the will – the *belief* – in an outcome to match an emerging spark, to welcome it, fill the gap with its certainty, we would have made good use of the universe and its powers. And to make good use of the universe is what we want here.

As I ate my curry noodles I had yet to come to an understanding of this idea, but in fact I had already seen it in action often enough: at the right moment, in the heat of a backgammon game for instance, or in the swirl of coloured silk at a racetrack. My feeling is that the heat of battle itself counts for something. The feverish state of belief we generate a few games into a series: bang – double six, bang – double four, bang – double six. Sure, there are times it doesn't happen but there are also times when I don't feel it will happen.

With this particular lottery ticket in my hand I couldn't afford to feel that I might fail. And to be clear, lest it sound like this was the only lottery ticket I'd ever bought: it wasn't. Not at that time. But it was the quantum model.

The draw was that evening and the balls pinged around their globe. At the press of a button they were slurped one by one from their cosmic chaos into a nozzle from which they bounced as numbered particles into reality.

The first came out – I had the first number!

The second – I had the second!

The third ball frisked and bucked in the nozzle.

Got it! Three numbers.

Ball four: I didn't want to look.

I got it.

Ball five: unbelievable.

Ball six: *bad luck.*

Five out of six, though. I could not believe it. Surely a fortune. I had no internet at the time so although I wanted to check the results again and again I couldn't. But I was sure I'd seen how the balls fell. To be fair the wins may not have fallen in the order above, but that's how it felt, bang, bang, bang.

It was night time so I walked up the highway to the service station to verify the win. It was a twenty-four-hour service station which had a terminal that could process the ticket when the results were in. In abandoning maths I must've also abandoned logic because I dreamt of the sandwiches I could buy from the chiller cabinet after the attendant cashed the win. But of course this would be too big a prize to pay out in a gas station. Easily tens of thousands, possibly much more, who knows. More likely the attendant would give me a receipt and I'd have to walk twenty miles to lottery headquarters in town because any bus money had gone on the ticket. Maybe he'd let me have a sandwich and a drink on credit. Maybe the ham salad roll. Maybe an iced coffee. Maybe I'd set off immediately and crunch along the gravel shoulder of the highway in damp night air, watch dawn light the city, watch aproned grocers manoeuvre crates of leafy produce as the last street sweeper hissed by. I knew it took time for results to be calculated. These were the thoughts that played in the meantime. I haunted the service station, browsing socket sets, batteries and engine oil as if I might buy them at two in the morning. The attendant indulged me with an air of having seen worse, and tried the ticket one more time.

Finally I had to give up for the night. Bad passive luck.

No results. By the next morning the service station had become part of the sacred cascade and I was compelled to return there to check the ticket. Plus there was the sandwich. So I presented there again and the results still hadn't come in. The ham salad roll was also gone from the cabinet. The morning rush had left the cabinet pretty bare, in fact. Reality was invading the day. I sucked it all up and after a while presented the ticket again.

This time the terminal pinged.

Results had finally come in but now a remarkable thing had happened: the number of people who had picked my same numbers must have been in the dozens or hundreds. It may have been a record. Forecourts across the land could've been crawling with strays clutching tickets. Ping-ping-*ping* – that's how luck travelled.

The payout was eight hundred bucks. A lucky win but not the win it would have been on any other week. It was actively lucky and passively unlucky, the superposition of a positive and a negative crashing together like waves at a cape. It was particle behaviour and the yield was eight hundred notes. Still I was grateful as hell and that little win floated me to the next level of all-or-nothing days, which floated me to the next again and eventually to here; that's the master cascade.

But luck as an event was very clear that day. It came not in one stroke but as a plot with three actors. Cast your mind back over strokes of luck and see if there didn't seem to be more than one thing going on, a positive-negative-positive action like pinball. A cascade. You're invited on a cruise – lucky! – on the *Titanic* – unlucky! – but you survive – lucky! – et cetera. Or an enemy drives off a cliff in your new car, or your wife gets pregnant but the father is your best friend. There are particles bouncing around in there flashing positive and negative at once.

On a book tour fifteen years later I went back to the same neighbourhood for the first time since that quantum apprenticeship. I went to the service station and it was all fancied up and new, but the newsagent looked just the same, bursting with fresh publications. You could smell it from the car park. By then I had some money so I finally perused those papers and magazines.

And I saw that I appeared in some.

A big snake was formed by the cascade.

Via Little Snake to this page.

And with this page that snake eats its tail.

The story at once has a moral, no morals and infinite morals. But sticking with Einstein: if we want a bird pepper tree we should put a bird feeder out with enough bird peppers in it that birds hang around for an hour and thirty-two minutes. And if we want to play a lottery we have to go out and buy the ticket.

If you're reading this at the newsagent you should do it *now*.

Big Snake

We were finally ready to shoot our short film with the parrot. My last task on the evening before was to collect some trays of sandwiches from a catering company. They were for the crew and five actors the next day. I brought the sandwiches home overnight but it wouldn't be for long, I was setting off before dawn to follow the van with the crew to the beach where we were going to shoot. Everything was set as I soared up the driveway.

A walled walkway surrounded half of this house, wrapped from the parking spot at the back to a main door around the side. The tiled walkway had a low metal gate at the entrance which was always closed and bolted. Arriving with a tray full of sandwiches I saw a big snake threaded between the gate's inner ironwork. A slim snake, not a boa. A biting snake. I stopped and looked at it and it looked at me. It had found a spot across the horizontal ironwork to twine and rest quite decoratively. Only the head and tail were self-supporting.

I took the sandwiches back to the car. It was late. I had barely four hours to sleep and set off to our shoot with these sandwiches. To spend the day on the beach directing our parrot. There was no other way to the door and I had no key to the service room at the back. To get to the door without confronting the snake would mean scaling a twelve-foot wall surrounded by low-lying thorny bushes.

Some snakes can fly. They coil and propel themselves to strike, such as the snake in my parents' cellar years before. I didn't know if this was such a snake. Once again I found myself watching a snake and it watching me back and both of us wondering what the fuck would happen next. What was also interesting is that I had prepared myself for encountering constrictors on the island. After stories of the anaconda that ate a man whole, all these *Jungle Book* snakes had primed the imagination, and I was ready for them. I was especially ready for an anaconda, and was confident of noticing one before it noticed me.

But a biting snake I was unprepared for. Undreamt-of risk.

Sleek aquiline biting snake. Perhaps a *mapipire*, as they call them, which is a pit viper. Perhaps some other kind of biting snake. I was about to enter into a game of roulette with a biting snake. Sandwich crusts rustled under their napkins behind me as the ingredients warmed and curled and sagged. I wondered if I should get back in the car and eat a sandwich, and simply wait for the snake to move on. Those sandwiches looked good, they had fresh Italian-style bread with ham and salad and cheese. The alternative was do I play roulette and try to shift the snake. The sandwiches needed to go in the fridge. I badly needed sleep. It was past midnight.

Back where the little parking spot met the coconut tree and the hill that rose behind, I found a large stick. I took it back and threw it at the gate, aiming for the right where it was hinged, to avoid hitting the snake directly.

It missed. Being a big stick, and bent, it had more of the properties of a boomerang than a baton, and it fell by the gate without clanging. The snake regarded me. And now the stick lay over by the snake. I couldn't see any other sticks around. The back porch threw light onto the parking spot and the coconut palm, and this was my area of focus. All around that was tall grass and jungle where you wouldn't risk rummaging in the dark for fear of another snake. I could throw the jack from the car but that would seriously piss the snake off. I needed to discomfit it, inconvenience it, not start a brawl. As it was he or she was halfway up to my eye level and six feet away.

I had to go and retrieve the stick. The odds were meanwhile shortening that the snake was at least increasingly suspicious, if not preparing to educate me once and for all. Already disturbed it flicked its tongue frantically, although that's what they do. As far as I knew, snakes don't do a lot before striking. And once they've reared up it can be too late. Especially with flying snakes. I cursed this fucking snake.

It would still be close to thirty degrees and Mosquito-Coast-level humid. I was sweating. You could hear the lettuce wilting in the sandwiches. Big slice of our budget due to film union rules, though of course I didn't begrudge the crew a sandwich, and would want one myself as well. But these were fancy sandwiches from a fancy catery place with fresh Italian bread in a clean little mall with air conditioning. Because we were a clean little crew full of cool clean people making a clean little film with a parrot. The snake was not of this narrative.

I took a couple of steps very slowly towards the gate. The snake watched but didn't move. I stepped a bit closer, crouching slightly to present less of a looming threat. I probably smiled at it. And finally, slowly, reaching, I took the tip of the stick between my fingers and quietly pulled it back out of range. Then I retreated to spend the few moments bomb defusers must spend after they cut the red wire and before they do or don't enter a tunnel of light. I finally breathed out, lobbed the stick again and it struck the gate.

The snake reared up. Flicked its tongue. But it didn't untwine its body in the least. Then I started to get the impression that this snake wasn't suspicious after all. That it didn't feel the least bit inconvenienced.

I now got the feeling, studying the snake, that it was just lazy. A welcome discredit to its species and its overall reputation as a fast sleek biting machine with a can-do attitude. The snake just liked the ironwork on the gate. It could hang and rest its weary bones. Expending its can-do attitude through its tongue. Now the paradigm shifted with the snake. Empathy flowed into the thick night air. The snake merely wanted what I wanted: to rest and stay out of trouble. With this realisation my pulse slowed back down and with that new calm came the real insight: it was another ping from the maths. The last snake on this walkway had been Little Snake. And it had been just as unperturbed, laying there on the doormat like a delivery left by a courier. But this one had even had the grace to climb on the gate where it wouldn't be missed in the dark. That's the level of special delivery we're talking about.

I stood and watched it. Now its scales seemed to glisten in the light. You could imagine it swallowing a smile that it was taking me too long to remember that I was living on an island of vivid maths. Big Snake: number thirty-five. Even Einstein would have placed that bet. And I would certainly play it.

But for now I had to get past Big Snake to enter the classical world of the fridge and the bed. So I crouched to retrieve the stick again. The snake was calm as I did this. I then found a spot on the same latitude as its tail, to the far right of the gate, over by the hinges; and I twanged the metal with the stick in a rhythmic way, not aggressively but rather like a harpist. A rhythm that set the whole gate vibrating, until the snake slid off and ran away over the concrete into the long grass.

By the time this had happened and both we creatures were finally in our respective, habitual places of rest, an hour must have passed. My sleep allowance for the big day out with the parrot fell under three hours. It meant the alarm went off within a quantum heartbeat of hitting the deck, and I scrambled to load up the sandwiches again. It was dark and windless outside.

Nowhere was open for Play-Whe on the route out of town. Surely we'd pass by a gas station on the way to the beach, or somewhere to play number thirty-five, Big Snake. But we didn't. I would have to send out a runner from the set.

But I didn't. The beach was remote and it would be an insulting waste of somebody's time in the everyday metrical world. We had a parrot to shoot and it took us past nightfall to make it back to town and unload.

I consciously avoided the Play-Whe result for that

evening. The result must still be discoverable even today, but in the meantime it remains a quantum win, though neither Einstein nor Hugh Everett nor I had a ticket, in this universe at least.

In reality the bet wasn't even half the point, the point was meeting the snake and remembering the maths. Connecting to the long cascade and its circus of symbols. That's where the vivid maths played out. Thinking about it, the snake itself was a cause of my not making it out of the house in an orderly way the next morning, thereby lengthening the odds of a win. It was another perfect example of particle behaviour: a snake came over – unlucky! – but it could be a vivid maths delivery – lucky! – but it took so long to shift that I didn't get out to buy the ticket – unlucky! et cetera. Vivid maths is the primal Jungian mentor.

As we've agreed: it was a snake and therefore could not be connected to games of chance in the metrical world, which dismisses recurrent symbolic agents manifesting out of nature. And we accept that.

But standing there in the glossy night air to the distant barks of dogs, to a wafting reggae from high up the hill, to fireflies sparkling like the subjective effects of a head injury – it could also be the opposite. Active and passive particles. And we accept that as well.

Little Snake confirms that since the big snake both was and wasn't connected to us, we – made of the same maths as it – are the sole deciders of that probability.

The Parrot Shoot

In a way the night before the shoot, night of Big Snake, had the action of an up-ramp of maths, a leading edge to new kismet, and a potentiator of forces for our caper on the beach. It was that herald of vibrant maths we often see at the start of our escapades, the ping-ping-*ping* that tells us conditions are live and active.

We should ask if in striking out on some caper – by definition always a universal first – our forward motion creates a bow wave, leaving behind us a turbulent wake of maths. Vigorous action in all other realms would do this, so why not our endeavours? If true it could also be a recipe to change our luck, a dynamic reboot: strike out in a random and different direction, set off from somewhere unknown, take detours without meaning, stir up the connections both inside and outside our heads.

We headed out before dawn towards Blanchisseuse, a stretch of northern coast so lush and clean that you crave to be shipwrecked there naked. The parrot film loomed and the big snake faded, though the crew agreed when I told them the story that I should have bought a Play-Whe mark. Some of them would have played it too, although that could have lessened my winnings. There was an instinctive sense that our cascades had converged and we now shared maths which included the story of the night before; the snake belonged to all of us.

And, should we win, even though we hadn't bet, the snake would become our myth. Our decisions to meet had sealed our fates and locked in the probabilities. This is how we feel that things roll. If the person beside us comes into luck we can shift our cascades and mingle with that self-same luck.

Passive luck was active on the parrot shoot as well. Our major passive concern had been the weather; it had been moody and rainy for some days before and we needed that to change. As morning broke and the coast approached conditions looked good enough; still moody but willing to listen. So we travelled with hope and the buzz of no sleep, while the catering seemed refreshed by its stay at the snake house. This was our condition as we hugged the island via the coast road, there being no direct route through the mountains of the Northern Range. The shoot was the business of a whole day long, what with travelling and production buzzwords and fresh Italian-style bread, plus wrangling a parrot.

The parrot was a little green star: a double-yellow-headed Amazon that would deliver the film's punchline at another shoot in a small studio, to add to a montage with the actors down at the beach. It was handsome, it had character, and with a wise-cracking smile on its beak it looked like it had character. It didn't escape me at the beach that I've always held parrots in high regard, always loved tropics, loved islands, loved undergrowth and oversized leaves and the scent of damp matting that goes with these places, and my attraction towards these things had resulted in their cascading all around me. This is how it works. Getting to the island was its own series of odds, some long, some shortened by action. Once there, gaining a position from which to require a beach with a parrot was a next set of odds. Finding the parrot and the beach and convening us here was the climax.

So we shot the bulk of our film and the parrot was resplendent on that small empty beach in a cove backed by palms and hanging lianas against a rockface, even a lagoon over a sand bar where we splashed after the shoot.

The crew were a new family. Actors were a new family.

Fresh Italian-style bread. Those odds kept shining down.

Amplified Risk in the Swamp

But there is a proven electrical frequency to humans. We radiate. Dogs can obviously pick it up. Ocelots, toucans and boas might get it. We can reportedly transmit to each other, but I'm not sure since we devised a system of language that we're in the habit of receiving so much anymore.

Now most transmissions are out of our mouths or over our screens, on a spectrum from wisdom to bullshit. And if we think about it most of our perceptions of risk, right or wrong, come from language and not from our senses. The palette of worldly risks has had a million colours added over the century behind us. Most of it second hand. Most of it on trust. Much of it delivered to the sound of trumpets and drums. Often for someone else's specific interest, and then probably financial. This is not to say that all stories of worldly risk are wrong but that between them in the mind they form a living landscape map whose holes and crags aren't drawn from life but are painted by numbers from a desk. The map is made topographical with soaring peaks and plummeting valleys via a value system created by news. Not everyone gets the same map and some are opposite. And we have to find our way through it. Are we more likely to get diabetes or crash the car? Who knows but we live, waiting. Proof of how badly the landscape is painted is that we spent that last century losing sleep over all the risks except for the urgent ones.

Another day on another road, two immaculately groomed colleagues were telling me about a pair of brothers who lived in the swamps and ruled a swamp fiefdom so brutal that no one who entered their territory ever came out. Same swamps of mangrove we've looked at already, with their big red birds and lurking risks and waters of fresh-laid glass.

They told me this as we passed by that swamp, with cane fields on the other side and the Northern Range behind us like the brow of Caerus, cleaving the maths in two as it blew to Venezuela. Ahead of us the curries were getting better and more rustic, the land was flat and bushy. You might spot vendors with bundles of mangrove hairy-crabs knotted together with rushes. And to the right were the brothers in their fiefdom of blood. As the story went they were so vicious that authorities would not go in to apprehend them, they were left alone to their feudal rule. The story's narrator sensed my interest and by now the story had it that the brothers had been raised as virtual savages.

I looked over at the swamp hoping to catch a glimpse. The shiver? But the brothers' cunning had stretched to not settling right beside the highway; one thing in the legend's favour. But they were in there somewhere, and I wondered what the risk would be of straying into their swamp kingdom. Both the swamp and the risk were big, and the problem was that it would be impossible to calculate the odds without at least some data from survivors, of which, according to the story, there were none. Now I could look this up and write a factual account but what was important here was the second-hand tale, the island myth.

What was happening with the swamp brothers' risk was that it was amplified by the legend alone. In fact, after completing this drive I learned that the brothers had lived there earlier in the century, they were in the past, they were not here now. But the perception of risk still existed. What if there were new brothers? Or sons or nephews or cousins? But in fact it didn't matter if there were or weren't new brothers or brethren or progeny because even when the original feral brothers were there, still nobody knew for sure. So that ninety per cent or more of the job of keeping people away from the swamp was achieved by the legend alone, and this story must have been repeated by locals every time anyone passed by the mangroves. I also couldn't see an appealing reason to go into the swamp, why would you go, except to tour nature on a boat; so whatever risk there was, which was incalculable anyway, wasn't worth taking.

The position for me is the position of the addicted gambler. Under the circumstance of feral brothers raised as savages ruling the area, there is no reason to go back into that swamp. The greatest reason for going back in is to experience the thrill of surviving to go back out; which is the thrill of the brain-chemistry of loss.

Again with a dusty smell of welling clouds through open car windows the island threw us up another model: how perceptions of risk can grip a place and hang beyond their time without being explored anymore. To put it in context, the only difference between the feral brothers and the link between saturated fats and death is that I think the feral brothers did at some point exist.

Dressing for Risk

The feral brothers occupy a place at the top end of a human spectrum describing how we dress for risk, as in what face we show it, what forces we exude to overcome that risk and dominate. At the feral brothers' end, according to the story we just heard from my immaculate colleagues, they would destroy, outright, any challenge on sight. While at the other end of the human spectrum most people would do nothing. Somewhere in between, probably just above the middle of the spectrum where the universe seems to like its eggs cooked, there must be an optimal attitude to show to risk. A best mindset.

Some time later four of us were sat at a table in a beer joint that was open to the street, one of those places where the floor and the street outside have most things in common. And a tall upright local man sashays in, brightly dressed, not young but not old, lucid and sharp. He sees us smoking and politely starts to pitch us a deal. We sense we're about to get worked over.

The man has charm and the deal is this: if he can launch a lit cigarette from his foot to his mouth and catch it the right way round, he gets to smoke it. Even before the trick is done we're impressed that it's not a straight beg but a risk taken, a contribution to the exhilarating languid leisure of a beer-joint table with a few of us sat around. The man talks us up, he works his crowd, there's a pitch but it's fluent, warm and at our level, and we accept the deal right away. So he takes off a shoe, lights the cigarette and slots it along his foot in a groove from his toes. He focuses like an athlete on the height and power requirements, looks up and down at the air. Then he tosses the smoke and it misses. The cigarette hits the floor.

We tell him to keep it but he's determined to finish the trick, so he tries again and this time the smoke finds his mouth. We cheer and he perches on one of our benches where we have the usual street exchange about where we're from and what joints we've been to. He doesn't stick around. By the time he leaves we know we were wrong for thinking he would work us over. He just needed a smoke. Then we see that our entire pack of smokes is missing from the table.

I recall this to bring one thing into focus: the man was operating with confidence of course, it was a confidence trick, an artform of risk – but he also had *the appearance of power-to-spare*. The scam was not only well within his power, he didn't care if it was or it was not.

And that seems a good model of how to face risk. He had mustered more force than the risk required, so much more that he would probably admit the scam, if he were ever caught in the act, and would still walk away with the smokes via some other means. If we're going to try it ourselves the appearance of power-to-spare has two essential components: we must downgrade the value of both the risk and the reward, while cranking our force of will to an apparently careless mastery. In the human world we tend to applaud the appearance of power-to-spare because it's above the vulgar simplicity of the feral brothers' technique. And I'd like to propose that the rest of the spectrum, including our best mindset, is coloured by fear, which restrains all endeavours.

Big fears and small fears, fears we're aware of and fears we're not, fear of losing and fear of winning, fear of who's watching and fear of who's not, fear of doing anything and fear of doing nothing. And probably nameless background fears as well. Not the fear of the feral brothers who at some time, in some way, were real and highly fearable, but fear of saturated fats. Fear of falling off the Earth. The end of the world according to the Mayan calendar.

The power of will we need to generate to meet risk and unlock vivid maths is suppressed by all our inherited fears. History is largely prompted by fear.

The vibes we give off seem to count for a lot across the natural world. And nothing pings clearer than fear, even that nameless background fear, a fear of being oneself or of simply being. For sure, the opposite is mindless arrogance which is an equal and probably quicker disaster, except in the hands of Trojan operators like the feral brothers; though remember they had a whole swamp to play with, which was half the winning equation – try being feral brothers in a suburb. But what's of interest to us is that the feral brothers' scorched-earth policies caused resistance by local people to their efforts. The swamp may have defeated the resistance but there was resistance nonetheless. And fear raises equal resistance, perhaps even stronger because it uses, lethally, insider information to encourage us to resist ourselves.

So the appearance of power-to-spare – which doesn't have to be a stable state across a lifetime but one we can generate in the moment, the right moment – might be, like the protein spike on a virus which unlocks the wealth of its host, a point of understanding and harmony with vivid maths. An agreement that our powers will hold sway for that instant.

In terms of gambles and the power to spare there are simple examples from the natural-history world of a casino I played in for a short good season with the mythical player Pike, who later appeared in my novel *Lights Out in Wonderland*.

We treated those nights seriously and even dressed for the occasion, going to a big glossy casino and playing blackjack, which gives the player the best odds of any game. We were so serious that we made a pact never to drink at the casino. It was unusual but that's how seriously we took it. We wanted to get to the bottom of vivid maths. A great friend also worked at the glossy casino, though naturally we didn't see him there, we couldn't appear to collude with him and anyway he was invisible as he worked back of house. But he had security access to the uppermost room in the place, a room where all the paintings on the walls were hung crooked. The uppermost room was the room you went to if a private jet had been sent to collect you in Shanghai at the casino's expense. The paintings hung crooked so that bad spirits couldn't gather on them, they would just roll off. The fact that the Chinese had such an instinctive romance with gambling gave me faith that there could be more behind it. The oldest, wisest, most collective of cultures could find something else at play here. A portal to the wider mechanisms of the universe. Vivid maths. That interested me and gave me an inkling that gambling isn't just about the money in and out, or if it is, that there was something else going on with that in and out. That the caprices of the universe flowed through the game, and when we played blackjack we paddled with them in a shallow.

As the casino hadn't sent a jet for us we played downstairs where the paintings hung straight. From the perspective of a blackjack table in a section adjacent to craps and roulette we got a sense of the manifestation of gathering forces. One example was a top-end twenty-something punter who was riding the thrill of early strong drink and was accompanied by some friends. They were all dressed up, and they were pointedly dressed up, probably on a big night out. Possibly a stag night. Haircuts and too much aftershave. Without an apparent care our player threw some money at the craps table, maybe his first of the night. His gang had come to the casino with him because it was louche and unwise and that resonated well with a big night out. So our lit-up player made two things known to all around: he was having a big, unwise bet, and he didn't give a fuck.

Naturally he won. Before even reaching this sentence you knew he would win. It sounds overly simple but think about it: we already knew but more importantly he already knew. He appeared to write the win into being, not by wishing but by knowing. He didn't come to create a win but to discover one. And this wasn't a phenomenon unique to him, it's such an accepted idea in casinos in every city that it's a universal trope. That night we saw it coming and it came. Our happy floater was lit up by his win which in turn lit us up too. The appearance of 'power-to-spare' never fails to excite, but it's a power that can vanish like swamp mist if it's observed too closely. People are grateful to even stand near it, and a small herd formed, as it will in a casino, around the man who knew he would win, that power flowed from him to us and back again and it made him know it more.

He wagered again, won again, and the halo grew around him. Then, without a care in the world, with the ease of stepping through an open doorway, he drifted brightly away with his crew. This was just one such player, you can find them every night from Monaco to Madrid. We utter strangers flashed brows, shook heads, rolled eyes but never said a word, we didn't have to: since every single player in that and every other gaming establishment the world fucking over knows that this bright performance used a specific energy which we all know exists and which we spend our lives trying to court for the purposes of general living, never mind winning at blackjack.

All the arguments we hear against this are from those who downplay the power. The numbers and the psychology that say the feeling and the outcome are unrelated in any way. And being good Einsteinians, we accept that.

But Little Snake asks us to accept that our forces and outcomes are connected.

The next sample was a similarly lit-up reveller with some friends who arrived at the same table on a different night. He was shrill, warbling and gurgling like a baby although he wasn't that drunk. It was a big night out and they came for a wager like James Bond, scrubbed like priests and with the rest of the trope in place. But this young man was a little too loud. A little too earnest. A little too jumpy.

As he threw his first bet he started to sing, 'Don't worry,

be happy'. And then he lost, and as he lost he warbled the lyric again in an ironic minor key. We knew he would lose, you knew he would lose, is the thing. You could see the trope coming round the corner – and *he* knew he would lose, and he lost. He sang and played and lost again until everyone wanted to kill him for singing that song, until he was busted. Then he finally went away. Minutes later through the velvety casino hubbub you could hear him singing the line again on his way out onto the street.

The joists of the issue: when Sample One came in with the appearance of power we expected he might win. When Sample Two started warbling we knew he had the fear and we expected he might lose. If on those two occasions I had bet on the outcomes of their bets, I would have won big. But it wouldn't have been a purely mathematical gamble – it would be a gamble based on the vibe they gave off.

As far as I could tell neither were regular gamblers.

When we bet on sport we are betting on skill. But craps are the original crapshoot.

Little Snake's casino hypothesis asks if people with power-to-spare exude a gravity, and if they do can they bend unfolding probability towards them just as magnets and planets pull objects into their orbit? Popular science would argue confirmation bias: that is, that we've established in our minds the trope of lucky ignorance and when we see it in reality we remember it above other outcomes as it confirms what we want to be true. And we're more likely to forget the instances where a lucky ignorant player loses.

But while we accept that confirmation bias exists, here's the thing: it still says nothing about our belief that forces and their outcomes are connected. The only reason we first thought they were unconnected was because we were told it at school.

All our information is second hand, and you sense that much of it could derive from the wisdom of long-suffering partners of gamblers in history. I sat around enough games of chance on the island to say I have never seen a worried player win by the end of the night. Let's try and be rational, cull some factors away: let's look at a gambler's specific strategy, for instance – the losers chase bad luck by increasing their bets and thereby losing faster. And fine, except we're talking about mathematical games and their win rates. It doesn't matter what a player's stakes are or how they're managed: if they're going to win they will win. And we're not talking best out of three; the longer cascade is something else. The winner could go elsewhere and become the worried player, it doesn't matter – we're talking about an affinity with one's own cascade of luck that bends and sways the outcome.

Aiming at the instant and not the longer game seems key. And perhaps this power-to-spare uses intelligence: the trickster at the beer shop didn't spend his day tossing smokes from his toes to his mouth.

He did it once and went for the whole pack.

Parrot Shoot 2.0

Power-to-spare is what the island blares. Day and night, here where the air is buttery and warm as breath, where afternoon rain can fall in firehose torrents and dry leaving a shine in time for the moonlight bacchanal.

Driving out to complete the parrot cascade with the last key shots in a studio I could taste the island as a whole; it had distilled to smoky spices and heat. When you can taste places whole, you sense you will always be able to close your eyes and savour them, but this thought often comes when you know you're having to leave. My season of vivid tropical maths would soon be over and the thought made everything richer, which is a way to live vividly by itself, the way of a wanderer; my favourite rusty freighter listing out in the gulf, favourite foods with their sudden *karela, pommes-cythère* or *chadon beni* or *shado beni* or *shadow benny,* depending on who you asked, all became sacraments in a new world of missing the place, or pre-missing it anyway, which they even have a word for here in Trinidad: *tabanca*. The island isn't a constrictor snake that ambles up to squeeze you, it's a biter and when it strikes you stay bitten.

What I especially loved was a human spectrum so diverse that the whole discipline of psychology got thrown out the door as there could be no 'normal'. Heading west along Wrightson Road, which skirts the coast in Port of Spain, there used to come a man prowling the kerb on all fours. He had a slow winding gait and was slim and hard as wood. His hair was a spiky shock like a wire brush and he was fully adapted in his limbs and joints for life on all fours. I learned there was a whole sub-stratum of these ragamuffins, which was the name I heard them called, and not without affection.

This man in rags was alert but uninterested in anyone passing by, he occupied a special place outside the realm of beggar where he was just not interested in money or favours. He may not have been able to speak, but he scavenged studiously instead. I was fascinated by him, he was a fellow human being, he seemed strong and healthy and, though many obvious social wrongs such as deprivation and disadvantage could be debated over cappuccinos, he seemed free.

Naturally by our standards the man was not free until he could aspire to a memory-foam bed and exercise his right to apply for restraining orders against the owner of the sofa warehouse who stalked his ex-fiancée before her parents broke the affair up with all their bullshit. Whereas look here, at the ragamuffin. He is saying 'fuck off'. To everything. He has adapted and is denizen of his state. He is not moved along by authorities. He is affectionately regarded by everyone. He wishes no harm and carries no burning dialogues over inverted abandonment issues, or losing the corner office. As far as I can tell he is free.

Nevertheless we're stuck with our standards so Little Snake tells us it's time to look at when cascades go bad. Cascades seem to establish a trajectory from their earliest momentum, their Big Bang moment; and seemingly like all travelling things they are most vulnerable at the beginning and end of their journey. Notoriously planes are in much more danger the closer they are to the ground. From our position the ragamuffin's circumstances took a dire early turn and kept heading that way till he roamed the gutters of town on all fours. However, if we had rescued the ragamuffin as a baby there's no guarantee that his cascade would not carry the harsh DNA of his birth.

It may also be that cascades come out bouncing like particles between positive and negative, as the savage ups and downs of many lives attest.

But this day we had a parrot to film which was its own cascade. We headed up Wrightson Road to the Audrey Jeffers Highway, driving west past Cocorite towards Carenage – 'Adios, Carenage', illuminated by Walcott's poem 'The Schooner *Flight*'. With our beach scenes in the can, and posters with the parrot already printed, we had made another date with the bird and its wrangler to get the last master shots. They agreed to accompany us in a van to a small house in the west of the island, an enclosed indoor-outdoor concrete patio in a concrete place where you could expect to see a clothesline hung with baby clothes. It also doubled as a studio and a few hundred dollars would change hands for these crucial seconds of film. We needed the parrot not only to behave but to perform; this was its big day out.

The parrot was in the van with us and we were intent on keeping it calm. Traffic would thin as we left the town behind, but meantime the bird didn't look particularly interested in the ride, it stayed affable enough, curling and bobbing its head around as they do. At Cocorite there was a service station where to kill time between customers one of the attendants made impeccable origami grasshoppers out of rush leaves. He gave me one once as a gift. Now, approaching that place with traffic either side of us, the parrot reacted to a honking horn in its ear. It flew up, found the few inches of open window by the front seat and flapped out.

What? We couldn't believe it. The bird escaped into the hustling traffic and then narrowly missed being hit by a rattling red pickup on the inside lane. This didn't improve its calm and it staggered on foot with its wings half aloft as our driver violently hit the brakes and tried to pull the van over. It was everyone for themselves on this road and we had pissed off a goods truck behind us. It floored the accelerator in retaliation and came barrelling down the inside. As we watched the bird make it to the gutter the truck carved between us and the kerb with barely enough room to spare. Our little green friend went up in a puff of feathers. Looking back it even seems as if the truck swerved up to the kerb to run it over.

Sickening twist in the cascade.

We got out and stood suppressing an instinct to gather the bird back up, go into the traffic and collect every feather.

We just stood and stared.

Parrot Jonah

Only much later it occurred to me: that was the third parrot I've lost or been associated with losing. Not distantly, not conceptually: parrots I've seen and touched. I've written before about one which flew away within a day of my receiving it. Before that there had been an unfledged chick called Pancho which I rescued from a market and raised till it was almost speaking; but it caught a virus that chicks catch and there was nothing we could do to save it.

Of those three parrots, two including the last one were lost after acting out of character against their wrangler's judgement. That very specific mechanism was activated twice. Bad, bad parrot cascade. And this wasn't like a hit rate of three out of ten, which would be gloomy statistics – this was three out of three. No odds at all.

I was the albatross to parrots and I should have stayed away from them all.

Cascades within cascades, wires twined in a cable, snakes

and ladders, up or down we go. Sub-cascades, cascadelets like open channels, and if you look at it we mostly know which ones they are. We call them 'situations' but no, they have heads and tails and are travelling somewhere with force. 'You shouldn't go in the bar, you know what always happens.' 'You shouldn't ping your ex, you know what always happens.' 'She never learns,' et cetera – all those statements speak of the cascades of events which may not be in harmony with their users.

Yet the user seeks them out. We try our luck again. There is something to gather and report on from our road trips with Little Snake, and it seems to support those ideas which propose that our belief in the probability of an outcome is itself a mechanism to power unfolding reality.

Look at the real problem with trying our luck again: where is the actual fucking border between good and bad luck? If there's a constant mathematical factor dictating that we cannot on average win ten out of ten or even seven out of ten times at anything, is that a faithful mirror of odds governing other processes in the universe? If probabilities are mathematical and the universe deals that maths it makes sense that it must be calibrated to a Middle C of odds. Raw luck must have a setting and is that setting high or low? That is: do we have to be massively lucky on average to feel we're any kind of lucky at all?

In Einstein's world we found ourselves with little more than a week to find an identical double-yellow-headed Amazon parrot. Trained, with a wise-cracking smile on its beak. As I say, posters had been printed. All the other footage had been shot with the tragic predecessor but the key shot was missing. Our budget was spent. We couldn't start again from scratch, least of all now after we'd paid a hefty sum – the most we could, and with sadness – to the boy wrangler for the bird's loss. If I could have started from scratch I would've left the parrot out. But that lethal cascade was determined, via my own natural attraction to parrots, to finish its course. Let's not even go into the theory that everything in reality has already happened and keeps happening ad infinitum. We are trying to have an innocent look at risk, not wipe out a species. So the vivid maths of the island that I was so strongly drawn to had shown us its power.

And this is where the cascade had left us.

Still, somehow conditions at this depth of it seemed to have changed. That one bad chance had stormed the cascade and quickly moved on like a cloud. For sure by now we were praying in earnest, visualising Amazon parrots in our sleep, even wondering if we might have to widen the net to South America to find one. But whereas finding the first had been like striking gold in a car park we now had a stroke of luck. Chance threw us up another Amazon parrot, also wrangled by a quiet boy from the boondocks. We could finally get our footage to Venezuela to be processed, at which a new cascade opened up which started with gunfire on the streets of Caracas; but that's a different story.

You just wonder, looking at it all, if our belief in how lucky we have to be could contribute to how lucky we have to be.

And how lucky we are. Look at our position in the universe: it has been calculated that if electrons were even one per cent larger or smaller than they are, we could not exist. It has also been calculated that in the ninety-three-billion-kilometre diameter of the observable universe – which some are now saying is only five per cent of it – there are thought to be two trillion galaxies with a few hundred billion stars each. And of all the ones we've looked at so far none is manufacturing sofas or currying ducks.

We don't know the total number of stars and planets and it's academic anyway because any light being sent from beyond twenty billion light years away will not reach the Earth; but the odds of our existence look extremely long. These are our primal odds. Our existence anywhere, ever, in any form, is governed by an extreme if not impossible set of odds. This is our starting point. Then we look up to the sky believing maths will dictate that we'll be averagely unlucky if we take another step? What shit is that?

I want to think the universe favours a belief in long odds.

The lifespan of an electron, once thought to be infinite, was recently trimmed down to sixty-six thousand yottayears, or around five quintillion times the age of the universe. One electron. Atoms contain between one and one hundred and eighteen electrons with corresponding protons, as well as neutrons and other crew.

An adult human comprises around seven octillion atoms.

That's   7,000,000,000,000,000,000,000,000,000   of them.

Each one contains particles with lifespans of five quintillion times the age of the universe. A snake, a boa, a bat, all comprise electrical matter with lifespans of at least five quintillion times the age of the universe, and some have also now been shown to be in two damn places at once. And there is no definition between the spaces between those atoms. No difference between our bodies and the die, our bodies and the table, the snake and the sandwich, no matter how solid they look. We are spaces dotted with varying designs and densities of matter with lifespans of five quintillion times the age of the fucking universe.

And I say there's room in there for some magic.

Be still and we can know it.

Some hours later the drinks wear off and this is revealed to be scientific.

But what if the science is real?

A-ha! says Little Snake.

And Then a Funny Thing Happened

Long cascades. It can be a hell of a job to try and unpick event-cascades looking back, as the cable of live reality in our hands is twined with so many wires, so many cascadelets, including in my case one reserved for parrots. But in terms of this island cascade, I was there long enough, and it was significant enough, to form part of life's main cascade. Looking back a little way we can trace the island cascade to not being able to get a job two years earlier. Zoom further back and we can trace my choice of this island to a book I read in my twenties – *Papillon* by Henri Charrière – which had a setting in Trinidad. Further back still I can trace that same copy to my parents' bookshelves throughout my childhood. I hadn't read it earlier because those bookshelves were a mental lightning rod for a notion I formed when I first grew aware of them that books without pictures may as well be school books, which were agents for the feeling that I had lost the will to live.

From even further back I can trace the entire cascade which saw me getting up to go to a chutney fête before midday to Bomber Harris and the Second World War where a young signals officer in Air Traffic Control gave the wrong directions to a bomber pilot. Those planes couldn't reverse, but her instructions to the pilot turned him onto an active runway where he faced another squadron preparing to take off with full bomb loads, destination: Germany. With engines roaring and precious fuel and nerves being spent it created a huge problem, forcing the airfield to shut down as ground crew were scrambled to tow the plane out of danger. It was so outrageous an error, with the war effort at such a fever pitch, and scores of pilots being lost every night, plus the young signals officer had been so snotty when the pilot queried the instruction – that he presented himself in person at the control tower to give her a piece of his mind; to which he later added his DNA and ended up with me making a lightning rod of his bookshelves.

This is what we're up against.

Cascades of action and chance driving the maths of breaking reality. And we are just on our meandering road trip. I'm still not a mathematician but I don't have to be to ask the questions; what you, Little Snake, and I tried to do was run a few scenarios through our minds in a different way to see what they threw up. Even as we spoke of maths it quickly became irrelevant as a practical tool in our inquiry. It retreated back into the jungle of theory, since we know there is currently no numerical answer to Little Snake. In other words we had to feel our way through this, and that's what we've done. Feel our way. Fuck the numbers. It seems impossible that we have survived three hundred thousand years as *Homo sapiens* without developing keen unspoken senses of emerging reality. More likely is that we had them and lost them the more affluent we grew. Chance and risk are our native climate and we are their agents of change. No amount of numbers can hide us from them.

And no amount of time can hide us from Little Snake. Because a weird thing happened just now as I sat writing. So far away from that place and time, the Little Snake cascade came to ping me in as live and affecting a way as the snake itself on that doorstep. The ping was even set off by snakes.

Check this: the work in here is light on research as it largely deals with memories and freestyle thoughts. Nevertheless I did look up snakes in Trinidad just now so I could at least name a species of biting snake. That quick research added *pit viper* to the text, not to say that Little or Big Snake was one. But I felt we should at least name some probabilities. Now together with *Trinidad* and *snakes* I added the word *biting* as a keyword in the search string. And surfing those results I also soon came upon vampire bats. I never knew there were vampires on the island but it wouldn't have mattered if I had known: vampires are countryside bats, you hear of them plaguing livestock. Anyway if there are boas, manatees and ocelots there may as well be vampires. Still I surfed some pages.

I surfed and read the most I ever had about vampires.

Some of it said this: the common vampire bat lives solely on the blood of warm-blooded prey, it doesn't even drink water. A vampire's saliva has anaesthetic and blood thinners to mask the bite and make a victim's blood flow. Victims don't feel the bite, so sharp are the teeth. Blood can flow freely for an hour after a bite, long after the bat has gone. Their little incisors are unenamelled and so sharp that cuts are even common in labs handling bleached display skulls. They're also the only bats that can walk, run and jump on the ground, so their flapping doesn't wake up sleeping mammals. There are videos of them creeping up as stealthily as cats, folding their wings to stalk their victims in silence.

I looked at the size and shape of them and remembered my house bat. The house bat wasn't one of your flying mice but a bigger type of bat, I thought maybe a fruit bat or something. I'd see it cruising at night through the gaps above the doors, it would enter high up near the ceiling, do a casual circuit through the room and fly back out. It had seemed that it lived there with me, and it was welcome to. I knew that bats are very accurate aviators, you don't hear of bat collisions.

But then looking at these vampire bats and remembering the gaps around the house, I thought: it would be longer odds for a bat seen indoors to actually be resident indoors. More probably the bat came in at random from outside. Which moved the odds again: it was less likely that it was the same returning bat. It could well have been many bats visiting one at a time on their patrol.

I kept surfing this topic and came upon some press articles from Trinidad. One carried the headline: *Vampire Bats Biting People Again*. The first line of the article read: *My great grandfather on his honeymoon was bitten by a vampire bat… He said he bled like a stuck pig*. I read on and discovered that there are plenty of vampire bats on Trinidad. And people get bitten. Trinidad is also the only Caribbean island with a history of rabies transmitted by vampires. Fifty-five people have died of rabies from vampire attacks in one outbreak to date. Obviously this won't happen at your hotel when you come to visit, nor necessarily at the house you rent with beige carpet and gaps between the walls and the ceiling on a jungled hillside. But it's more likely at the house with the gaps. So then – picture this dawning on me now like a haemorrhage – I found reports of an outbreak of vampire attacks at the time I was there. Exactly the time I was there.

The language in these reports wove itself into my dawning: *high numbers of human-bat interactions; folks once regarded the bites as a nuisance, even a badge of honour; bats in this area were not afraid of humans …*

And it came to me:

The soucouyant.

My blood-soaked pillow.

And I thought: wow.

Ping! Fuck.

Hello Little Snake.

Bonjour vivid maths.

Dedications

For Spottie and the cricket tour that kicked off this cascade.

To my padnas who brought the probabilities to life: Steve, Keith, Carol-Ann, Diana, Simone, Christine, Carol, Lystra, Paulina, Caryl, Kirtlee, Mark, Nathan, Khaleel, Sean, Lightning Fox, Marlon, Junior, Cox, Timmy, Ali, Mac, Richard, Curtis, Major Peter and all yuh who's give me *tabanca*.

And

to

Clare,

Harriet,

Darren,

Rachel

for

grabbing

the

snake

by

the

tail.